Religion Within Reason

Second Edition

Religion Within Reason

Second Edition

STEVEN M. CAHN

RESOURCE *Publications* · Eugene, Oregon

RELIGION WITHIN REASON, SECOND EDITION

Copyright © 2025 Steven M. Cahn. All rights reserved. Except for brief quotations in critical publications or reviews, no part of this book may be reproduced in any manner without prior written permission from the publisher. Write: Permissions, Wipf and Stock Publishers, 199 W. 8th Ave., Suite 3, Eugene, OR 97401.

Resource Publications
An Imprint of Wipf and Stock Publishers
199 W. 8th Ave., Suite 3
Eugene, OR 97401

www.wipfandstock.com

PAPERBACK ISBN: 979-8-3852-4204-7
HARDCOVER ISBN: 979-8-3852-4205-4
EBOOK ISBN: 979-8-3852-4206-1

VERSION NUMBER 02/24/25

Where indicated Scripture translations have been taken from New Revised Standard Version Bible, copyright © 1989 National Council of the Churches of Christ in the United States of America. Used by permission. All rights reserved worldwide.

I. L. Peretz, "If Not Higher," trans. Marie Syrkin, from *The I. L. Peretz Reader*, ed. Ruth R. Wisse, copyright c 2002. Used by permission of Yale University Press.

In memory of my parents,

Rabbi Judah Cahn and Evelyn Baum Cahn

Contents

Preface | ix

1. Proving God's Existence? | 1
2. Philosophical Proofs and Religious Commitment | 6
3. The Problem of Evil | 10
4. The Problem of Good | 14
5. The Moriarty Hypothesis | 17
6. Dummy Hypotheses | 20
7. The Appeal to Faith | 24
8. Skepticism About Faith | 27
9. The Theodicy Trap | 32
10. The Problem of Meaning | 36
11. Miracles | 40
12. God Without Religion | 44
13. Playing the Odds | 47
14. Why Worship God? | 50
15. Religions | 57
16. Religion Without God | 60
17. Heaven | 68
18. Life Without God | 72
19. A Religious Life | 78

Works by Steven M. Cahn | 85
About the Author | 91
Index | 93

Preface

In *Stardust Memories*, a 1980 movie written and directed by Woody Allen, the protagonist, Sandy Bates, meets a strange-looking creature named Og, who along with others of his kind have arrived in a spaceship from Mars. Presuming that Og has superhuman knowledge, Sandy asks him: "Why is there so much human suffering?" Og replies, "This is unanswerable." Then Sandy tries again, "Is there a God"? Og responds, "These are the wrong questions."[1]

This exchange might appear to lead to a dead end, but in this book I argue to the contrary that Og's answers suggest that the key to understanding the human condition does not lie in an appeal to supernaturalism. Religion can be a valuable aspect of our lives but not by leading us to suppose we can explain the inexplicable. Indeed, adherence to religion does not require belief in God, and belief in God does not require adherence to religion.

This framework for my discussion will not lead me away from reviewing familiar topics, although in doing so, I shall raise unfamiliar questions, consider unusual examples. and suggest uncommon conclusions. In other words, we shall travel well-worn roads but attend to sites that are not often noticed.

I recognize that in recent decades, skilled philosophers defending central tenets of Christianity have developed a voluminous technical literature. Equally proficient critics have found these arguments unpersuasive. Such debates are not my focus here, as I hope to redirect attention elsewhere.

---

1. *Four Films of Woody Allen* (New York: Random House, 1977), 366.

PREFACE

The first edition of this book was published about a decade ago by Columbias University Press, and the kind reception the work has received leads me to offer this second, expanded edition.

For numerous stylistic suggestions, I am grateful to my brother, Victor L. Cahn, playwright, critic, and professor emeritus of English at Skidmore College. I am also indebted to Dr. Mary Ann McHugh, instructor in the Hugh Downs School of Human Communication at Arizona State University, for her elegant polishing of the entire manuscript. To my wife, Marilyn Ross, MD, I owe more than I would try to say.

This book is dedicated to my father from whom I learned to ask philosophical questions about religion and to my mother, a beloved high school teacher of English, who was devoted to Judaism as were her father, the eminent cantor Solomon Baum, her mother, Victoria Bieber Baum, a font of practical wisdom, her eldest brother, Lester, who served as a New York State Senator, and her elder brother, Morton, who for many years was responsible for the programming and finances of the New York City Center of Music and Drama. My mother's family exemplified religious commitment within reason, the approach with which I myself am most comfortable.

I

Proving God's Existence?

DESPITE MY NOT BELIEVING that religious commitment and belief in God are interdependent, I shall begin with a brief survey of the traditional arguments for the existence of God. They can be formulated and defended in a variety of ways, but I shall bypass innumerable complications to focus on a straightforward version of each.

First, though, we need to clarify what is meant by the term *God*. The word has been used in various ways, ranging from the Greek concept of the Olympian gods to the proposal by John Dewey that the divine is "the active relation between ideal and actual."[1] Let us adopt the more usual view, common to many religious believers, that *God* refers to an all-good, all-powerful, all-knowing, everlasting creator of the world. The question, then, is whether a being of that description exists. A theist affirms that claim, an atheist denies it, and an agnostic believes the matter as yet undecidable. Which of these positions is the most reasonable?

We begin with the cosmological argument, which rests on the assumption that everything that exists depends for its existence on something else. For example, a house results from the actions of its builder, and rain results from certain meteorological conditions.

---

1. John Dewey, *The Later Works of John Dewey, 1925–1953*, vol. 9, ed. Jo Ann Boydston (Carbondale: Southern Illinois University Press, 1988), 34.

But if everything that exists depends for its existence on something else, then the world itself depends for its existence on something else, and this "something else" is God.

Although the cosmological argument may seem initially plausible, it has a major difficulty. If everything that exists depends for its existence on something else, then God also depends for existence on something. In that case, the world's existence would not depend on God, for God is supposed to be all-powerful, not dependent on anything else.

A defender of the cosmological argument might try to surmount this difficulty by claiming that God is self-explanatory, that is, the reason for God's existence lies within God. But even if we admit that any series of explanations needs to stop at some point (although the mathematical notion of an infinite series suggests otherwise), the cosmological argument nevertheless crumbles, for if the world's existence depends on something that is self-explanatory, why cannot the world itself be self-explanatory? In that case, no need would arise to postulate something on which the existence of the world depends because the existence of the world would itself be self-explanatory.

Furthermore, even if God were self-explanatory, no connection would have been established between God and human concerns. What difference would it make to our lives if a self-explanatory being existed?

A second classic proof for the existence of God is the ontological argument. It makes no appeal to empirical evidence but purports to demonstrate that God's essence implies God's existence. In its simplest form, the argument assumes that God possesses all perfections. Then on the grounds that a being who exists is more perfect than one who doesn't, the conclusion is that God must exist.

Although this argument has been defended in subtle ways, it is open to the crucial criticism, stated succinctly by Immanuel Kant, that existence is not an attribute. In other words, the definition of anything remains the same regardless of whether that thing exists. For example, the definition of a unicorn would not be altered if we discovered a living unicorn, just as our definition of a whooping crane would not be altered if whooping cranes became extinct. In short, whether unicorns or whooping cranes exist does not affect the meaning of the terms *unicorn* and *whooping crane*.

To clarify this point, imagine a ferocious tiger. Now imagine a ferocious tiger that exists. What more is imagined in the second case than the first? Our concept of a ferocious tiger remains the same whether any ferocious tigers exist.

Applying this insight, we see a major difficulty with the ontological argument. Because the definition of something remains the same whether it exists, the definition of God remains the same whether God exists. Thus, existence cannot be part of the definition of God. God may be understood to possess every perfection, but existence does not render something more perfect because existence is no attribute at all. To assert that something exists is not to ascribe perfection to the thing but to state a fact about the world. What we mean by God is one matter; whether God exists is another. The ontological argument conflates the two and thereby seems to go awry.

The third argument we shall consider, the teleological argument, is much less abstruse. Its defenders point out that the world possesses a highly ordered structure just like an extraordinarily complex machine. Each part is adjusted to the other parts with wondrous precision. For instance, the human eye, which so many of us take for granted, is a mechanism of such intricacy that its design is breathtaking. But doesn't a design require a designer? The magnificent order of our world cannot be a result of chance but must be the work of a supreme mind responsible for the order. That supreme mind is God.

Although this argument has persuasive power, it suffers from several critical difficulties. To begin with, any world would exhibit some kind of order. Were you to drop at random ten coins on the floor, they would exhibit an order. An order, therefore, does not imply an orderer. If we use the term *design* to mean "a consciously established order," then a design implies a designer. But the crucial question is the following: Does our world exhibit mere order or a design?

If the world were just like a machine, as the teleological argument claims, then because a machine has a design and a designer, so would the world. But is the world just like a machine? David Hume in his *Dialogues Concerning Natural Religion* suggests that our experience is too limited for us to accept such an analogy. Philo, the skeptic in the *Dialogues*, notes that although the world bears some slight resemblance to a machine, the world is also similar to an animal:

> A continuous circulation of matter in it produces no disorder: A continual waste in every part is incessantly repaired. The closest sympathy is perceived throughout the entire system: And each part or member, in performing its proper offices, operates both to its own preservation and to that of the whole.[2]

Cleanthes, the rational theist in the *Dialogues*, adds that the world is also somewhat like a vegetable because neither has sense organs or brain, although both exhibit life and movement.

The key point is that whereas any machine requires a designer, animals and vegetables come into being differently from machines. Hume is not suggesting that the world came into being as does an animal or vegetable, but he wishes to demonstrate that the world is not sufficiently like an animal, a vegetable, or a machine to permit us to draw reasonable conclusions from such weak analogies. Lacking them, the teleological argument appears to collapse for we have no reason to believe that the world exhibits design rather than mere order.

As Philo points out, however, even if we were to accept the analogy of world and machine, the argument remains unconvincing. Let us grant, he says, that like effects prove like causes. Then if the world is like a machine, the cause of the world is like the cause of a machine. Remember, however, that machines are usually built after many trials; so the world was probably built after many attempts. Machines are usually built by many workers; hence,

---

2. David Hume, *Dialogues Concerning Natural Religion and Other Writings*, ed. Dorothy Coleman (Cambridge, UK: Cambridge University Press, 2007), 6:3

the world was probably built by many deities. Those who build machines are often inexperienced, careless, or foolish; therefore, the gods, too, may be inexperienced, careless, or foolish. Perhaps this world "was only the first rude essay of some infant deity, who afterwards abandoned it, ashamed of his lame performance." Or perhaps "[i]t is the work only of some dependent, inferior deity; and is the object of derision to his superiors." The world might even be "the production of old age and dotage in some superannuated deity; and ever since his death, has run on at adventures, from the first impulse and active force which is received from him."[3] By suggesting such possibilities, Hume demonstrates that even if we grant an analogy between the world and a machine, and further agree that both were designed. we are not thereby committed to believing that the world's design is the work of one all-good, all-powerful, all-knowing everlasting designer.

What, then, is the source of order? The world may have gone through innumerable structural changes until a stable pattern was reached, and the existence of such complex phenomena as the human eye may be a result of the process of natural selection whereby surviving forms of life are those than can adjust. Such an explanation of the world's order not only requires no recourse to the hypothesis of a supreme designer but has also been confirmed by biological research since the time of Charles Darwin.

I conclude, then, that none of the three best-known arguments for the existence of God is satisfactory. Might one of the arguments be developed in a version more plausible than any I have suggested? I would not be surprised, but rather than adding to the immense philosophical literature devoted to attacking or defending proposed arguments for God's existence,[4] let me consider a different question: Are religious believers deeply concerned with whether the existence of God can be proved by a philosophical argument? Probably not, and I want to explain why their attitude is reasonable.

3. Hume, 5:12.

4. For balanced readings on this topic and others I discuss, see my *Exploring Philosophy of Religion: An Introductory Anthology*, Second Edition (New York: Oxford University Press, 2016).

2

Philosophical Proofs and Religious Commitment

GIVEN THE EMPHASIS PHILOSOPHERS have placed on trying to formulate a proof of God's existence, one would suppose that religious believers are vitally interested in such efforts, enthusiastic when a proof is persuasively defended and seriously disappointed when one is refuted. Such, however, is not the case. Indeed, religious believers seem remarkably uninterested in the subject. They apparently consider discussion of such proofs to be an intellectual game with no relevance to religious belief or activity. For example, the heterodox Danish existential philosopher and theologian Søren Kierkegaard remarked, "Whoever therefore attempts to demonstrate the existence of God...[is] an excellent subject for a comedy of the higher lunacy."[1] The same essential point was made in a less flamboyant manner by Rabbi Mordecai M. Kaplan, who noted that the "immense amount of mental effort to prove the existence of God...was in vain, since unbelievers seldom become believers as a result of logical argument."[2] Both these thinkers, while nontra-

---

1. *Philosophical Fragments,* tr. David F. Swenson (Princeton: Princeton University Press, 1936), III, 34.

2. *The Future of the American Jew* (New York: The Macmillan Company, 1948), 171.

ditional, are correct in their common contention. After all, have you ever heard religious believers explain that their commitment resulted from having found a convincing version of the ontological argument?

In what follows I wish to explain why religious believers have so little interest in intricate arguments. I believe that this lack of concern is reasonable and that whatever the philosophical significance of technical arguments for the existence of God, they have little relevance to religion.

Suppose we assume, contrary to what most philosophers believe, that the three classic proofs for the existence of God are all sound. Let us grant the existence of the most perfect conceivable being who is the designer of the universe. What implications of this supposition would be relevant to our lives?

Some people would feel more secure in the knowledge that the world had been planned by an all-good being. Others would feel insecure, realizing the extent to which their existence depended on a decision of this being. In any case, most people, out of either fear or respect, would wish to act in accord with God's will.

Belief in God by itself, however, provides no hint whatsoever of which actions God wishes us to perform or what we ought to do to please or obey God. We may affirm that God is all-good yet have no way of knowing the highest moral standards. All we may presume is that whatever these standards, God always acts in accordance with them. We might expect God to have implanted the correct moral standards in our minds, but this supposition is doubtful in view of the conflicts among people's intuitions. Furthermore, even if consensus prevailed, it might be only a means by which God tests us to see whether we have the courage to dissent from popular opinion.

Some would argue that if God exists, then murder is immoral because it destroys what God with infinite wisdom created. This argument, however, fails on several grounds. First, God also created germs, viruses, and disease-carrying rats. Because God created these things, ought they not be eliminated? Second, if God arranged for us to live, God also arranged for us to die. By killing, are we assisting the work of God? Third, God provided us with the mental and physical potential to commit murder. Does God wish us to fulfill this potential?

Thus, God's existence alone does not imply any particular moral precepts. We may hope our actions are in accord with God's standards, but no test is available to check whether what we do is best in God's eyes. Some seemingly good people suffer great ills, whereas some seemingly evil people achieve happiness. Perhaps in a future life these outcomes will be reversed, but we have no way of ascertaining who, if anyone, is ultimately punished and who ultimately rewarded.

Over the course of history, those who believed in God's existence were typically eager to learn God's will and tended to rely on those individuals who claimed to possess such insight. Diviners, seers, and priests were given positions of great influence. Competition among them was severe, however, for no one could be sure which oracle to believe.

In any case, prophets died, and their supposedly revelatory powers disappeared with them. For practical purposes, however, what was needed was a permanent record of God's will. This requirement was met by the writing of holy books in which God's will was revealed to all.

But even though many such books were supposed to embody the will of God, they conflicted with one another. Which was to be accepted? Belief in the existence of God by itself yields no answer.

The only direct, unmistakable avenue to the divine will is an experience in which one senses the presence of God and apprehends which, if any, of the putative holy books is genuine. To be certain, however, that you are experiencing God's presence and apprehending God's will, the experience cannot be open to error, for only then can it provide an unshakeable foundation for religious commitment.

If one undergoes such an incorrigible experience, it guarantees which holy book is genuine and consequently which rituals, prayers, and actions God authorizes. Note, most importantly, that such an experience by itself validates the existence of God, for unless God's presence has been experienced, the message may not be true. Thus, any further proof of God's existence is unnecessary. For someone who does not undergo what is believed to be a genuine experience of the divine, several possibilities remain open. The individual may accept another person's claim to have had such an experience, thereby accepting any holy book that has been revealed and also accepting the existence of God, because unless this other person has experienced God, the report could be mistaken.

Suppose, though, that you do not accept someone else's report of an experience of God. This unwillingness may be due either to philosophical doubts concerning the possibility of such an experience (an issue to be discussed later) or practical doubt that anyone has ever undergone such an experience. In either case, adherence to a particular view of God's will is unreasonable.

Consequently, most religious believers have little concern about proofs for God's existence. After all, if the proof is sound, it merely confirms what is already known on the stronger evidence of someone's personal experience. If the proof is unsound, it does not undermine the impact of such experience. In either case, religious experience trumps philosophical proof.

3

The Problem of Evil

THE FAILURE OF A philosophical proof for the existence of God does not by itself prove that God does not exist. To reach that conclusion requires a separate argument, and a much-discussed one is the problem of evil. The Greek philosopher Epicurus, as cited by Hume,[1] puts it most succinctly: Is God willing to prevent evil, but not able? Then God is impotent. Is God able, but not willing? Then God is malevolent. Is God both able and willing? From where, then, comes evil?

In other words, an all-good God would do everything possible to abolish evil. An all-powerful God would be able to abolish evil. Hence, if an all-good, all-powerful God existed, evil would not. But evil exists. Therefore, an all-good, all-powerful God does not.

While most theists exhibit little concern about proofs for God's existence, they take much more seriously a proof for the non-existence of God, because if such a proof is plausible, it casts doubt on the reliability of any experience of God, which is the only path toward the knowledge of God's will.

Hence, numerous attempts have been made to provide a defense of God's goodness in the face of evil, a project known as a "theodicy," derived from the Greek words *theos* and *dike* meaning

---

1. Hume, 10:25.

"God" and "goodness." A promising approach, offered by the English philosopher and minister John Hick,[2] begins by distinguishing two types of evil: moral and physical. Moral evils are those for which human beings are responsible, such as murder, theft, and oppression. Physical evils are those for which human beings are not responsible, such as typhoons, locusts, and volcanic eruptions.

Moral evils are justified by the hypothesis that God has given us free will, the power to do good and the power to do evil. Which we do is up to us. God could have ensured that we always act rightly, but had God done so, God would have had to eliminate our free will because a person who is forced to act rightly is not free. God is all-powerful but cannot perform an act whose description is contradictory, for such a supposed act is no act at all. For example, God cannot create a square circle, but God's inability to do so is no limitation on God's power, because by definition a circle cannot be square. Similarly, God cannot create free persons who must always act rightly, because by definition a free person is one who does not always have to do what is right. God, therefore, had to choose between creating beings who always did what was right and creating those who were free to do both right and wrong. God chose the latter because it constituted the greater good. Thus, all moral evils are justified as necessary concomitants of the best possible world God could have created, namely, a world in which people can do good freely.

Physical evils are justified by their providing the opportunity for human beings to develop moral attributes. If the world were a paradise without hardships and dangers, people would be unable to acquire the strength of character that results from standing firm in the face of difficulties. The world was not intended as a pleasure palace but as an arena of "soul making" in which human beings grapple with their weaknesses and in so doing acquire the strength that will serve them well in some future life.

Hick defends his position further by employing what he terms the "method of negative theodicy." Suppose, contrary to fact, the

---

2. John Hick, *Philosophy of Religion*, Fourth Edition. (Englewood Cliffs, NJ: Prentice Hall, 1990), 39–48

world were arranged so that nothing could ever go badly. No one could harm anyone else, no one could perform a cowardly act, and no one could fail to complete any worthwhile project. Presumably, such a world could be created through innumerable acts of God, who would alter the laws of nature as necessary.

Our present ethical concepts would thereby become useless. What would fortitude mean in an environment without difficulties? What would kindness be if no one needed help? Such a world, however efficiently it promoted pleasure, would be ill-adapted for the development of the best qualities of the human personality.

Hick emphasizes that this theodicy points forward in two ways to life after death. First, although we can find many striking instances of good resulting from evil, such as dangers that produce courage or calamities that develop patience, in many cases, evils lead to selfishness or disintegration of character. Thus, any divine purpose of soul making in earthly history must continue beyond this life to achieve more than a fragmentary success.

Second, if we ask whether the business of soul-making is so good as to offset the evils we find, theists need to answer in terms of a future good, such as heaven, that is great enough to justify all that has happened. Otherwise, the evils of our world are inconsistent with theism.

Does this two-pronged reply to the problem succeed in blunting its force? Yes, to some extent. Those who pose the problem may claim the logical impossibility of an all-good, all-powerful God permitting the existence of evil. We have seen, however, that under certain circumstances an all-good, all-powerful God might have to allow evil to exist, for if the evil were a logically necessary component of the best possible world, then God, wishing to bring about that world, would have to utilize whatever evil was necessary for the achievement of the goal. In other words, if the good was impossible without the evil, then the evil would be required to achieve the good. In that case, a world containing evil might have been created by an all-good, all-powerful God.

Yet how likely is the hypothesis that we live in the best possible world whose evils are logically necessary for the good? Do the greatest of tragedies and horrors enhance our lives? Are we better off because of them? How plausible, after all, is Hick's theodicy? Let us test it by considering the effectiveness of a similar approach to an analogous issue I call "the problem of good."

4

The Problem of Good

SUPPOSE SOMEONE WERE TO claim that the world was created by an all-powerful, all-evil Demon. That hypothesis could be challenged by the problem of good. Succinctly stated, the problem is this: Could a world containing good have been created by an omnipotent, omni-malevolent Demon? To adapt the reasoning of Epicurus: Is the Demon willing to prevent good but not able? Then the Demon is not omnipotent. Is the Demon able but not willing? Then the Demon is not omni-malevolent. Is the Demon able and willing? From where, then, comes good?

In other words, an all-evil Demon would do everything possible to abolish good. An all-powerful Demon would be able to abolish good. Hence, if an all-evil, all-powerful Demon existed, goodness would not. But good does exist. Therefore, an all-evil, all-powerful Demon does not.

Surprisingly, we can develop a reply to the problem of good along the same lines suggested by John Hick's response to the problem of evil. We begin by distinguishing two types of goodness: moral and physical. Moral goods are those for which human beings are responsible, acts such as altruism, generosity, and kindheartedness. Physical goods are those for which human beings are not originally responsible, such as sunshine, breathable air, and drinkable water.

The justification of moral goods proceeds by tying their existence to our free will. Surely, performing a bad act freely is more evil than performing it involuntarily. The Demon could have ensured that human beings would always perform bad actions, but then those actions would not have been free because the Demon would have ensured their occurrence. Simply performing them, therefore, would not have produced the greatest possible evil because greater evil can be produced by free persons than by unfree ones. The Demon had to provide human beings with freedom so that they might perform their bad actions voluntarily, thus maximizing evil.

As for the justification of physical goods, we should not suppose that the Demon's purpose in creating the world was to construct a chamber of tortures in which the inhabitants would be forced to endure a succession of unrelieved pains. The world can be viewed, instead, as a place of "soul breaking" in which free human beings, by grappling with the exhausting tasks and challenges in their environment, can thereby have their spirits broken and their wills-to-live destroyed.

This conception of the world can be supported by what, following Hick, we may call "the method of negative justification." Suppose, contrary to fact, the world were arranged so that nothing could ever go well. No one could help anyone else. No one could perform a courageous act. No one could complete any worthwhile project. Presumably, such a world could be created through innumerable acts of the Demon, who would alter the laws of nature as necessary.

Our present ethical concepts would thereby become useless. What would frustration mean in an environment without hope? What would selfishness be if no one could use help? Such a world, however efficiently it promoted pain, would be ill-adapted for the development of the worst qualities of the human personality.

This justification, like that of Hick, points forward in two ways to life after death. First, although we can find many striking instances of evil's being produced from good, such as the pollution of beautiful lakes or the vandalism of great paintings, in many other cases, good leads to altruism or strengthening of character. Therefore, any demonic purpose of soul breaking at work in earthly history must continue beyond this life to achieve more than a fragmentary success.

Second, if we ask whether the business of soul breaking is so evil that it offsets all the goodness we find, the demonist (the analogue to a theist) needs to answer in terms of a future evil, such as hell, that is great enough to justify all that has happened. Otherwise, the goods of our world are inconsistent with demonism.

Does this two-pronged reply to the problem of goodness succeed? Yes, to some extent. Those who pose the problem may claim the logical impossibility of an all-evil, all-powerful Demon permitting the existence of good. We have seen, however, that under certain circumstances, an all-evil, all-powerful Demon might have to allow good to exist because if the good were a logically necessary component of the worst possible world, then the Demon, wishing to bring about that world, would have to utilize whatever goodness was necessary for the achievement of that goal. In other words, if evil was impossible without goodness, then goodness would be required to achieve evil. In that case a world containing good might have been created by an all-evil, all-powerful Demon.

Yet how likely is that situation? Does anyone find plausible that the beauty of a sunset somehow contributes to a worse world? Or that the free will of Abraham Lincoln achieved greater evil than would have been produced by his performing evil actions involuntarily? No more convincing is Hick's proposal that the horrors of bubonic plague somehow contributed to a better world. Or that the free will of a Stalin achieved greater good than would have been produced by his performing right actions involuntarily. None of these suppositions is believable.

Thus, although the problem of evil and the problem of good do not demonstrate the impossibility of either the existence of God or the existence of the Demon, these problems show both doctrines to be highly improbable. If theists or demonists can produce any other evidence in favor of their positions, then they might increase the likelihood of their views, but otherwise, the reasonable conclusion is that neither God nor the Demon exists.

5

The Moriarty Hypothesis

THE SUPPOSITION THAT THE world was created by an all-powerful, all-evil Demon may appear strange. Yet perhaps even stranger is the realization that its defenders may have the same expectations about the events of this world as do theists. In other words, both demonists and theists may choose to interpret their contrary views as supported equally by any future occurrences, no matter how good or evil they may be.

To illustrate this admittedly counterintuitive claim, consider the fictional examples of Sherlock Holmes and his archenemy, Professor Moriarty. Holmes believed that Moriarty was the "great malignant brain" behind crime in London, the "deep organizing power" that unified "every deviltry" into "one connected whole," the "foul spider which lurks in the center," "never caught—never so much as suspected."[1] Now suppose Moriarty's power extended throughout the universe, so that all events were the work of one all-powerful, all-knowing, all-evil Demon. Let us call this theory "the Moriarty hypothesis."

Does the presence of various goods refute the Moriarty hypothesis? No, for, as we have seen, just as any good can be viewed

---

1. Arthur Conan Doyle, *The Complete Sherlock Holmes* (Garden City, NY: Doubleday, n.d.), 471, 496, 769. The works cited are "The Final Problem," "The Adventure of the Norwood Builder, and "The Valley of Fear."

as logically necessary for a greater evil, so any evil can be viewed as logically necessary for a greater good. Thus, the Moriarty hypothesis is not obviously false.

Now consider the following two assessments of the human condition:

1. "Is not all life pathetic and futile? We reach. We grasp. And what is left in our hands at the end? A shadow. Or worse than a shadow—misery."
2. "The first entrance into life gives anguish to the newborn infant, and to its wretched parent; weakness, impotence, distress attend each stage of that life, and it is, at last, finished in agony and horror."

Which is the viewpoint of a theist and which that of a believer in the Moriarty hypothesis? As it happens, (1) is uttered by Sherlock Holmes,[2] and (2) by the orthodox believer Demea in Hume's *Dialogues Concerning Natural Religion*.[3] The positions appear interchangeable.

Neither the theist nor the believer in the Moriarty hypothesis need deny that life contains happiness as well as misery. No matter how terrible the misery, the theists may regard it as unsurprising; after all, aren't all evils, in principle, explicable? To believers in the Moriarty hypothesis, happiness may be regarded as unsurprising; after all, aren't all goods, in principle, explicable? Supporters of both positions are apt to view events that appear to conflict with their fundamental principles merely as tests of fortitude, opportunities to display strength of commitment.

If defenders of either view modified their beliefs in the light of changing circumstances, then their expectations would differ and their views would be subject to change in the light of circumstances. But believers are loath to admit doubt. They admire those who stand fast in their faith, regardless of appearances.

---

2. Doyle, "The Adventure of the Retired Colourman," 1113.
3. Hume, 10: 8.

Any seemingly contrary evidence can be considered ambiguous. St. Paul says, "[W]e see in a mirror, dimly,"[4] while Sherlock Holmes speaks of seeking the truth "through the veil which shrouded it."[5] If events are so difficult to interpret, they provide little reason for believers to abandon deep seated tenets. Those who vacillate are typically viewed by other members of their communities as weakhearted and faithless.

One other attempt to differentiate the expectations of the theist and the believer in the Moriarty hypothesis is to suppose that theists are necessarily more optimistic than their counterparts. This presumption, however, is unwarranted. Recall the words from the Book of Ecclesiastes: "Then I accounted those who died long since more fortunate than those who are still living; and happier than either are those who have not yet come into being and have never witnessed the miseries that go on under the sun."[6] A more pessimistic view is hard to imagine.

We may be living, as the theist supposes, in the best world God could have created, but if so, it contains immense torments. On the other hand, we may be living, as the believer in the Moriarty hypothesis supposes, in the worst world the Demon could have created, but if so it contains enormous delights. Both scenarios offer us reason to be cheerful and reason to be gloomy. Our outlook depends on our personalities, not our theology or demonology.

Thus, as we seek to understand life's vicissitudes, does it matter whether we believe in God or the Moriarty hypothesis? Not if we hold either of these beliefs unshakably. For the more tenaciously we cling to either position, the less significant is its content.

---

4. I Corinthians 13:12 NRSV.

5. Doyle, "The Final Problem," 471.

6. Ecclesiastes 4:2–3. The translation, as all subsequent ones from the Hebrew Bible, is from *Tanakh: The Holy Scriptures* (Philadelphia: Jewish Publication Society, 1988)

6

Dummy Hypotheses

To HOLD TO AN explanation of events in the face of conflicting facts is not to protect one's view but to render it pointless. As an illustration of this principle, consider the following anecdote found in Anita Shreve's novel *All He Ever Wanted*:

> A man is propelled one minute sooner to his automobile because he decides not to stop to kiss his wife good-bye. As a consequence of this omission, he then crosses a bridge one minute before it collapses, taking all its traffic and doomed souls into the swilling and angry depths below. Oblivious, and safely out of harm's way, our man continues on his journey.[1]

Let us first suppose this man is a theist who, once aware of his good fortune, attributes it to the benevolence of God. What are we to make of his claim?

To begin with, whatever goodness God displayed in this man's case did not extend to the many others who fell to their death. How is God's benevolence compatible with such a tragedy? Our man does not know, but when he ponders the matter, he is likely to suppose that the chain of events serves a divine purpose that lies beyond human understanding.

---

1. Anita Shreve, *All He Ever Wanted* (Boston: Little, Brown and Company, 2003), p. 79.

Suppose next that this man does not believe in the existence of God but, instead, accepts the Moriarty hypothesis, thus attributing events to the malevolence of the Demon. What are we to make of this claim? Obviously, whatever evil the Demon displayed in these horrific events did not extend to the man himself, for he was saved. How is the Demon's malevolence compatible with this man's good fortune? He does not know, but when he ponders the matter, he is likely to suppose that the chain of events serves a demonic purpose that lies beyond human understanding.

A third hypothesis the man might accept is that the world is the scene of a struggle between God and the Demon (or as Zoroastrians view it, a cosmic war between Ahura Mazda, the source of all good, and Ahriman, the source of all evil). Assume both God and the Demon are powerful, but neither is omnipotent. When events go well, God's benevolence is in the ascendancy; when events go badly, the Demon's malevolence is in the ascendancy. In the tragic case under consideration, the Demon caused the collapse of the bridge while God arranged for the one man to be saved.

Is this third explanation unnecessarily complex and therefore to be rejected? No, for even though in a sense it is more complex than the other two because it involves two supernatural beings rather than only one, in another sense the third explanation is simpler than the other two because it leaves no aspect of the situation beyond human understanding.

The crucial point is that all three hypotheses (as well as innumerable others one might imagine) can be maintained regardless of the facts. For instance, suppose the bridge had collapsed at a time when all vehicles but one had already crossed. The theist would thank God for having saved the lives of so many while considering mysterious why the one vehicle was lost. The believer in the Moriarty hypothesis would attribute the loss of the one vehicle to the work of the Demon while considering mysterious why the lives of so many were saved. The believer in both God and the Demon would thank God for having saved the lives of so many while attributing the loss of the one vehicle to the work of the Demon.

Any of these incompatible hypotheses can be interpreted to account for whatever events occur. Using them in this way turns them into dummy hypotheses, compatible with all possible facts. Like a dummy bell rope that makes no sound, a dummy hypothesis makes no sense. Its compatibility with all possible situations robs it of any explanatory power.

Contrast a dummy hypothesis with a scientific one, which is typically tested by the following four-step procedure: (1) formulate the hypothesis clearly; (2) work out the implications of the hypothesis; (3) perform controlled experiments to verify whether these implications hold; (4) observe the consequences of these experiments and as a result accept or reject the hypothesis. In practice, complications may abound at each stage, and any of the assumptions made for the purpose of the experiment may be challenged. Furthermore, the method yields only high probabilities, not certainties, for a hypothesis may pass numerous tests yet fail additional ones. The crucial point, however, is that scientific hypotheses are tested, then rejected if inconsistent with the outcome of the tests.

As an example of how scientific method works, consider the case of the American army surgeon Dr. Walter Reed, who sought to control yellow fever. He hypothesized that the disease was caused by a specific type of mosquito. To test his hypothesis, he divided his participants into two groups: a control group, quarantined to prevent contact with the insects, and a test group, deliberately exposed to the mosquitos. When the test group developed the disease and the quarantined group did not, Reed had strong evidence that mosquitoes caused the disease.

Had the results of the experiment been different, Reed's hypothesis might have turned out to be false. If those quarantined had developed the disease at the same rate as those exposed, then Reed would have rejected his hypothesis and been led to develop and test others.

That a hypothesis can be disproved by testing is not a weakness but a strength. Any genuine hypothesis is open to possible refutation. Dummy hypotheses are not and thus do not provide understanding. They may be psychologically comforting but do not enable us to gain control over our environment.

Some may choose to attribute an outbreak of yellow fever to God or the Demon or a struggle between them. Such hypotheses are untestable, and, therefore, do not help eradicate or control the disease.

Finally, a few thoughts about the story of the fallen bridge with which we began. Why did it collapse? The answer is most likely to be found by calling in engineers who can determine the cause, learn from the case, and build a new bridge that will be safer. At no point, however, will they rely on theories involving divine or demonic beings.

Yet some may persist in asking why the one man was saved. The answer is that he arrived one minute sooner because of not stopping to kiss his wife good-bye. Why didn't he kiss his wife good-bye? Perhaps he was distracted by thoughts of an upcoming business meeting. Why was that meeting so critical? We can continue such speculation endlessly, but the key point is that no question we may raise will be answered satisfactorily by appealing to any dummy hypothesis.

7

The Appeal to Faith

FEW THEISTS VIEW THEIR belief in God as resting on a scientific assessment of empirical data. Rather, they see themselves as persons of faith, firm in their convictions regardless of any apparent evidence to the contrary. I have already suggested the pitfalls in disregarding facts that conflict with one's beliefs, but here I want to focus directly on the nature of faith and offer another example to clarify further its potential dangers.

To have faith is to put aside any doubts, and doing so is sometimes beneficial because doubt may be counterproductive. Golfers who doubt they will hole their putts are likely to miss them. Teachers who doubt their students' ability to learn are less effective instructors. A crucial component of achievement is perseverance, and those who doubt themselves may be less likely to persist in the face of difficulty or opposition. In short, certitude often correlates with success, whereas doubt is apt to lead to failure.

To describe someone as a person of faith suggests that the individual is strong-willed, fearless, and unwavering. To describe someone as a person without faith suggests that the individual is weak-willed, fearful, and faltering.

Faith, though, can be misplaced. If you are not an experienced mountain climber but set out to scale Mount Everest because you have faith in your ability to succeed, then you are reckless. If your supposed friend routinely betrays your confidence but you continue to have faith in this individual, then you are gullible. If you have faith in your ability to master the violin in ten lessons, then you are ignorant.

Thus, faith in the sense of assurance can be wise or foolish. The circumstances of the case make the difference. Faith, however, in the sense of an unwillingness to acknowledge evidence contrary to one's beliefs is unwise and may prove disastrous.

Consider a fictional clairvoyant named Sibyl, who is asked to help in the search for a missing friend of yours. After undergoing a trance, Sibyl emerges to announce that your friend can be found in a place where darkness dwells. Subsequently, your friend is found tending bar in a Manhattan nightclub. Sibyl's followers acclaim her insight because, as they point out, a nightclub dwells in darkness.

You are impressed with Sibyl and recommend her to someone else searching for a lost cousin. Sibyl is consulted, and after undergoing another trance, emerges to announce that the cousin is to be found in a place where darkness dwells. Subsequently, the cousin is found on Cape Cod. Sibyl's followers again acclaim her insight because, as they point out, recently the weather on the Cape has been rainy and the skies dark.

As it turns out, whenever Sibyl is consulted regarding a person's whereabouts, she announces that the individual is in a place where darkness dwells. Regardless of the outcome of subsequent searches, her followers acclaim her insight and interpret her prediction so that it conforms with the outcome of the search. If the person being sought is no longer living, that individual surely dwells in darkness, while if the person cannot be located, that individual has vanished into darkness.

Are Sibyl's predictions true? Are they false? They are neither, for they are consistent with all possible situations and thus useless, wholly without significance. Because the place darkness dwells can turn out to be any place, Sibyl's words do not identify any particular site or eliminate any possibilities. In other words, she has offered a dummy hypothesis. Her followers may find that she provides them with psychological comfort. In a crisis, however, paying close attention to her pronouncement and attempting to act on it could be fatal.

Suppose a man is kidnapped. Every minute counts. Hearing from Sibyl's admirers of her reputation for helping to find missing persons, the police consult her and, unsurprisingly, she tells them that the victim is to be found where darkness dwells. If the police spend any time trying to decipher what she says and search where she is suggesting, all may be lost, for as we know, even if the police do not, her words provide no clue to any particular location.

A similar problem undermines the claim that a certain occurrence is in accord with God's plan, or in accord with the Demon's plan, or in accord with the struggle between God and the Demon. After all, whatever happens can be understood as in accord with any of these plans. Such plans are no plans at all, and having faith in any of them is akin to having faith in Sibyl's predictions.

Believing in God's providence may provide theists with a sense of calm during trying times. In a medical emergency, for example, those who have faith in God may find that prayer helps them deal with the stress of the situation. Before taking time to pray, however, theists are well advised to seek the services of a reliable physician. For even though having faith in God may offer some the best chance to ease worry, relying on science offers all the best chance to achieve health.

Faith also opens the door to intolerance. If the majority hold a particular faith and are unwilling to be proven wrong, what may be the consequences for a minority? Will the majority permit the minority to believe differently even if certain that the minority's beliefs are mistaken?

The historical record is not encouraging. If my belief can be wrong, then your opposing belief can be right, and I am inclined to listen to your arguments. If my belief, however, cannot be wrong, then your opposing belief cannot be right, and I have no need to take account of your concerns. Indeed, I may set out to save you from your errors. Thus arises persecution, carried out in the name of the good but inevitably leading to a reign of evil. For even though a faith may lack meaning, its adherents may not lack malice.

8

Skepticism About Faith

IN THE PREVIOUS CHAPTER, I presumed that belief in God might provide theists with comfort, giving them a sense that all is well even when evils occur. As said in a Hebrew prayerbook, "[I]n the fullness of time we shall know why we are tried, and why our love brings us sorrow as well as happiness."[1]

Surprisingly, a powerful challenge to such faith is found in the Bible itself. The Book of Job, in particular, although commonly misinterpreted as a defense of faith in God, suggests instead that the more we know of God's intentions, the less they justify God's actions. This scriptural story constitutes a challenge to theism, asking why bad things happen to good people.

Consider the plot. After a short introduction in which Job's exemplary piety and extraordinary good fortune are described, the scene shifts to heaven, where a dialogue takes place between God and Satan. God proudly comments to Satan about Job's remarkable spiritual qualities. Satan scoffs at Job's devoutness, claiming that Job is obedient only because God has given Job good health, a fine family, and untold wealth. Although God testifies to Job's genuine piety, God permits Satan to test Job by inflicting on him the severest personal losses. Suddenly, all ten of Job's children die, and his

---

1. *The Union Prayerbook*, pt. I (New York: The Central Conference of American Rabbis, 1958), 151.

wealth is destroyed. When Job does not relinquish his faith in God, Satan, claiming that Job has maintained his faith only because his own body has been spared, obtains further permission from God to inflict on Job a most painful disease.

The scene now shifts to the land of Uz, the place of Job's residence. Having heard of his misfortunes, Job's three friends, Eliphaz, Bildad, and Zophar, come to comfort him. Job vents his feelings of despair, cursing the day he was born and avowing that under his circumstances, death is better than life. Eliphaz advises Job to calm himself and not despise the chastening of the Almighty. Eliphaz believes that because Job is suffering, he must have sinned, for God does not punish the innocent. Eliphaz also counsels Job to repent for his sins and be restored to God's favor.

In response, Job points out that Eliphaz has not understood Job's outburst. He has not lost faith in God. Rather, Job longs for death because his life has become intolerable. In a harsh rejoinder, Bildad tells Job that God does not pervert justice and that if Job were upright, he would be prosperous. Job once again pleads with his friends that they do not understand the point of his complaint. He recognizes, as they do, the majesty of God, but Job claims to be innocent. He wishes only to know in what way he has erred, so that he might wholeheartedly repent. Finally, Job cries out that he would willingly present his case before God if the Almighty would only provide the opportunity.

The three friends and a newcomer, Elihu, repeat Eliphaz's basic argument: Job is suffering and therefore a sinner, but if he would repent of his sins, God would pardon him. Job's response continues to be that although he claims innocence, he is prepared to be judged and, if found guilty, accept just punishment.

The climax of the story comes when God answers Job from out of a whirlwind. God speaks of God's own wisdom and power in the creation and control of the mighty forces of nature. God points out the utter insignificance of humanity in the presence of God. God then questions Job's right even to inquire of God, for how could humanity ever hope to understand the workings of the Almighty? Finally, God urges Job to renew his faith in the wisdom, goodness, and justice of God, even though Job cannot hope to understand their workings.

In the divine presence, Job is overawed. He humbles himself before God, promising never to inquire of God again but forever to believe fervently in the greatness and power of the Lord. The story concludes as God rebukes Eliphaz, Bildad, and Zophar for the advice they gave Job, pardoning them only out of regard for him. God heals Job, restores to him twice as much wealth as he had possessed before his misfortunes, and blesses him with ten children and a long and happy life.

Now let us examine the traditional interpretation of the Book of Job, which views it as a defense of God's power, knowledge, and goodness as well as an admission of human ignorance regarding the divine. Here is one such account:

> The Book of Job teaches us that God's ways are beyond the complete understanding of our little minds. Like Job, we must believe that God, who placed us in this world, knows what is best for us. Such faith in the goodness of God, even though we cannot altogether understand it, brings us strength and confidence to face our calamities and sorrows and sufferings.[2]

And another:

> The total mystery of God can be gleaned from the Book of Job. There we are presented with a deity whose workings in nature can in no way be inferred from a knowledge of nature's order. For how did that order come into existence? That is God's secret. Nor can man's moral intuitions be trusted. Job *knows* he is innocent, yet in the end he is satisfied to accept the dictate that the conventional-minded friends with whom he has carried on a courageous, honest debate are in a sense correct. Who is he, a mere mortal, to challenge God's justice? There is infinitely more to it than even his clear conscience can hope to fathom. Indeed, he cannot any longer allow himself to think of God as just or unjust, at least as these

---

2. Mortimer J. Cohen, *Pathways through the Bible* (Philadelphia: Jewish Publication Society of America, 1946), 460.

terms are understood by man. These categories have no meaning when applied to God.[3]

Again:

> The positive contribution of the Book of Job comes in the "Speeches of the Lord," which give Job something better than that which is provided by the feeble remarks of his friends. The essential point of these final speeches is that the problem is too great for the finite mind, that Job sees only a small segment of reality, and that his criticisms are accordingly inappropriate. How can Job *know* that either God's power or goodness is limited? Job's knowledge of temporal things is admittedly slight; his knowledge of eternal things is still more slight. The conclusion of the book is Job's recognition of his own humble status with the consequent mood of childlike trust.[4]

All these variations on the theme of our not understanding the ways of God overlook a key passage: the opening dialogue in heaven. If this scene were eliminated, the traditional understanding of the book would be persuasive. Readers would be in the place of Job. They would not know why he was suffering and would, like Job, be overawed by God's appearance from out of the whirlwind.

But readers are not in this position. We were told explicitly at the outset of the story why Job would suffer. Satan had, in effect, made a wager with God about the strength of Job's faith, and the wager required Job's suffering. God's words from out of the whirlwind at the climax of the plot appear childish when we are, in effect, behind the scenes. For God to have answered Job's question truthfully would have shown God to be anything but a great moral force. Does a righteous being make a wager involving human lives? Thus, much in in the manner of the bully who, when engaged in a philosophical dispute, challenges opponents to a fistfight to settle the issue, God attacks Job's position *ad hominem*,

---

3. Jack J. Cohen, *The Case for Religious Naturalism* (1958; Eugene, OR: Wipf and Stock Publishers, 2019), 83.

4. David Trueblood, *The Logic of Belief* (New York: Harper & Brothers, 1942), 293–94.

trying to disallow Job's right to ask an embarrassing question by emphasizing his inability to control nature.

Job does not possess God's power, but Job's question remains unanswered. Job may be overawed, but readers should not be, for we are aware of the circumstances surrounding God's actions. God's ways may be beyond Job's understanding, but they are not beyond that of the reader. We can hardly be expected to have "childlike trust" in the goodness of a God who not only punishes Job unfairly but kills his ten children without any possible justification. Had these individuals done anything wrong? Their lives were sacrificed as part of the wager. The ten children who are given to Job at the end of the story may to some extent compensate Job for his previous losses, but are the dead children compensated? Are they restored to life?

What, then, is the significance of the Book of Job? It stands opposed to the prevailing theology of almost all the rest of the Hebrew Scriptures. The doctrine of retributive justice, as presented in Deuteronomy, Psalms, Proverbs, and elsewhere, states that a pious person will be rewarded with wealth and happiness; a sinner will suffer both economic and physical adversity. Traditional believers supposed that the righteous were favored by God with material rewards, whereas sinners were punished with calamities.

The Book of Job is a criticism of this theology. Later thinkers, however, could not accept this protest. They tried to twist the text into a pattern of orthodoxy. In effect, they turned a challenge to the righteousness of God's justice into a defense of unquestioning faith.

The Book of Job does not justify God's ways; rather, it doubts God's goodness. The Book does not provide support for faith in the divine. To the contrary, it offers powerful support for skepticism about such faith.

9

The Theodicy Trap

THE BOOK OF JOB calls for the development of a more plausible theodicy than any we have found. Yet even if one could be proposed, a major problem would remain.

Any theodicy is shaky if it explains only some evils but not all. For if certain evils are inconsistent with the existence of God, then their occurrence would disprove God's existence. Experience makes all too clear, though, that if an evil is possible, then it likely has occurred. Thua, a successful theodicy needs to offer a justification for all evils. Only then is theism secure.

Suppose, for example, an earthquake happens, killing thousands. Some might suppose that such an event would undermine belief in an all-powerful, all-good creator of the world. With a successful theodicy in hand, however, theism would be safe from refutation by such an event; its occurrence could be explained without limiting the power or goodness of God. But would such a successful theodicy afford believers any comfort? Perhaps not.

For example, Psalm 23 refers to God as our shepherd. Even as "I walk through a valley of deepest darkness, I fear no harm, for You are with me."[1] But why shouldn't I fear harms? They may befall me even if I am in God's care.

1. Psalm 23:4.

Perhaps comfort is supposed to be found eventually in a next world, although that comfort, as we shall see later, is at best obscure. As to this world, though, not only can bad things happen to good people, and good things happen to bad people, but the most wonderful things may happen to the worst people, and the worst things may happen to the most wonderful people. A successful theodicy envisions and justifies all these possibilities, thus destroying any reason to be hopeful about events in this world.

Consider an analogous case. Suppose I recommend a restaurant, praising it for the excellence of its management. During your visit, though, you find the ambience gloomy, the service poor, the food unpalatable, and the cost high. When you express disappointment about your visit, I present a complicated argument proving that all these conditions are consistent with the management's excellence. Indeed, I even show that these conditions are to be expected in such a restaurant. You may not know how to refute my chain of reasoning, but the next time I recommend a restaurant on the basis of its management, you won't be eager to eat there. After all, my view that excellent management is consistent with an inferior dining experience implies that you have no reason to suppose that conditions at a restaurant with such management will be in any way satisfactory.

Similarly, if God's plan for the world is consistent with a succession of the worst evils, you have no reason to suppose that conditions in the world need ever be in any way satisfactory. A drought, for example, might persist for years, while a successful theodicy would provide a justification for the continuing oppressive condition. Moreover, praying to God for rain in those circumstances appears to make little sense, for if the drought is justified, why should God stop it?

To highlight this problem, consider another well-known theodicy, that offered by Richard Swinburne. He assures us that God's plans require "much evil." Like Hick, Swinburne views moral evils as necessary for free will, but he presses this point by arguing that my suffering as a result of your freely chosen evil action is not entirely a loss for me because I have contributed to the cause of freedom. "Those who are allowed to die for their country and thereby save their country from foreign oppression are privileged." Thus, according to this theodicy, being the victim of injustice has a good side, even for the victim.

As for natural evils, Swinburne maintains that they give us the opportunity to perform worthy acts. Pain, for instance, helps develop patience. Thus, injustice contributes to the good not only as a by-product of free choice but also as an effective means for victims to develop moral virtue.

Swinburne's theodicy is so powerful that it implies not only that our world would be worse without evils, but that heaven would be better if it contained evils. In fact, Swinburne doesn't hesitate to draw this conclusion. He notes that heaven "lacks a few goods which our world contains, including the good of being able to reject the good."

No wonder that, in reflecting on his theodicy, Swinburne warns, "I would not in most cases recommend that a pastor give this chapter to victims of sudden distress at their worst moment, to read for consolation. But this is not because its arguments are unsound; it is simply that most people in deep despair need comfort, not argument."[2]

Swinburne recognizes that his theodicy offers no comfort. The crucial point, however, is that no successful theodicy does; it justifies whatever events occur.

The sad fate of some is to suffer through years filled with unrelenting woes. An effective theodicy would demonstrate that such wretched lives, no matter how common, do not conflict with belief in an all-powerful, all-good God. If they did, then theism would fall prey to the problem of evil. A successful theodicy would solve that problem but leave believers without any reason to expect support from God.

In that connection, recall the moving words of the Levite benediction:

---

2. Richard Swinburne, *Is There a God?* (Oxford and New York: Oxford University Press, 1996), 96, 102, 113.

> The Lord bless you and protect you!
> The Lord deal kindly and graciously with you!
> The Lord bestow His favor upon you and grant you peace![3]

A successful theodicy would prove that even with the Lord's blessing and protection, the Lord's kindness and graciousness, and the Lord's favor, your life on earth may be filled with evils, and you shouldn't expect God to alleviate them. After all, that theodicy has demonstrated that whatever evils occur, God views them as contributing to a greater good.

If this conclusion is unacceptable to theists, one way out would be to cease searching for a theodicy, continuing instead to conceive God as all-good but recognizing God's power as limited. In that case, facing a pandemic, for instance, theists could perhaps find some comfort in the realization that God wished to provide immediate relief, even if not able to do so. Moreover, praying to God would still be appropriate, although God could not grant every legitimate request.

Admittedly, this account of God's nature would likely appeal to few theists. By accepting it, however, they could abandon the implausible claim made by every successful theodicy that God considers all evils, including pandemics, to be enhancements of life.

---

3. Numbers 6:24–26

10

The Problem of Meaning

To explain why a world created by an all-good, all-powerful God contains so much evil, theists are tempted to respond that the reasons are known to God but not to us, for we lack the intellectual powers to grasp God's plans. In the words of one of the commentators on the Book of Job whom I quoted previously, "God's ways are beyond the complete understanding of our little minds."

To deny *complete* understanding of God, however, is a dodge because we may not completely understand anyone, even ourselves. What we seek is at least partial understanding of God. Do we possess it?

To assert that we do reopens the problem of evil, for even a partial understanding of God should include a partial understanding of evil, a burden theists don't wish to shoulder. After all, who is prepared to offer even a partial explanation of how the best possible world contains the massive slaughter of innocents? The sure way to avoid the question is to deny any understanding of God. To adopt this position, however, is fatal to theism. How can we make sense of the view that something exists if it is a total mystery?

Suppose, for instance, we are asked whether we believe in the existence of a "snark."[1] We inquire what a snark is, what specific

1. I take the term from Lewis Carroll's humorous poem "The Hunting of the Snark: An Agony, in Eight Fits," reprinted in *Alice in Wonderland*, ed.

THE PROBLEM OF MEANING

characteristics it possesses. If we are told its nature is unknowable, what would be the sense of our affirming or denying its existence? About what would we be talking? Belief in the existence of a wholly incomprehensible snark is empty. So is belief in the existence of a wholly incomprehensible God.

To avoid this pitfall, theists may claim that we do have some knowledge of God's nature because, for example, we know God is wise and just, although the words wise and *just* have a different meaning when applied to God than when applied to human beings. What is this meaning? One possible answer is that no one knows. Yet this reply leads to a dead end, for we cannot speak intelligently using words we don't understand. If the meaning of the words we apply to God is unknown, then so is God.

One traditional response to this difficulty is to maintain that God's attributes cannot be conceived in positive terms but only negatively. For example, to say that "God knows" is to deny that God does not know. This approach is supposed to make possible the avoidance of applying human concepts to the divine essence.

But to deny that someone does not possess knowledge is to affirm that the individual does possess knowledge. If that implication fails to hold, then we do not understand the meaning of our own words, and we cannot use them to make meaningful claims.

If God's knowledge has nothing in common with human knowledge, then, as the medieval Jewish philosopher Levi ben Gershom, known as Gersonides, argued: We might as well say that God lacks knowledge, adding the proviso that the term *knowledge* applied to God does not have the same meaning as it does ordinarily.[2] In other words, once we allow ourselves to use words without being able to offer any explanation of them, we might as well say anything, for none of what we say makes any sense.

What if the words we apply to God are to be taken not literally but metaphorically? Does that approach help deal with the problem? Only if the metaphors can be explained in non-metaphorical

---

Donald J. Gray (New York: Norton, 1971), 213–30.

2. Levi ben Gershom, *The Wars of the Lord*, trans. Seymour Feldman (Philadelphia: Jewish Publication Society, 1987), 2:111.

language. Otherwise, we are attempting to elucidate a mystery by means of an enigma.

To see how a normal metaphor can be unpacked, consider an example offered by Janet Martin Soskice, who developed a sophisticated defense of the use of metaphor in speaking of God. Commenting on e. e. cumming's line "nobody, not even the rain, has such small hands," she proposes that "the power of the metaphor rests in its casting up in the reader's mind thoughts of what kinds of hands rain might have, suggestions of fragility, delicacy, transience, ability to reach the smallest places." Thus does Soskice intend to show that a metaphor may offer "a new vision, the birth of a new understanding, a new referential access."

She stresses that science as well as literature uses metaphor. In both cases, the figure of speech arises from a model, which she defines as "an object or state of affairs viewed in terms of its resemblance, real or hypothetical, to some other object or state of affairs." The brain may thus be modeled on a computer, leading to talk of "programming," "inputs," and "feedback."

If, however, theological models are analogous to scientific ones, shouldn't the former, like the latter, be causally explanatory, falsifiable, and revisable? Soskice agrees, arguing that "the Christian realist must concede that there is a point, theoretically at least, at which he would be committed to surrendering his theism."[3] Where is this point? The question is invariably left unanswered.

In offering her account of the line by e.e. cummings, Soskice explains its metaphor in non-metaphorical language: The rain is delicate and transient. If that rain is part of a hurricane, then the claim is false.

Can theological metaphors also be explained so as to yield non-metaphorical claims? If so, we can speak of God literally, a position theists typically seek to deny.

If the metaphors cannot be explained, however, why is one more appropriate than another? We speak of God the Father or God the Mother. But why not God the Aunt or Uncle, God the

---

3. Janet Martin Soskice, *Metaphor and Religious Language* (Oxford: Clarendon Press, 1985), 57–58, 101, 140.

Cousin, or God the Neighbor? Some may protest that these phrases are inexplicable. Perhaps so. But one inexplicable metaphor is as good as another.

Thus we are left with the problem of meaning. How can we describe an incomprehensible God?

11

Miracles

IF WE CANNOT MEANINGFULLY speak of God, can we at least experience the working of God's will? Do some events bear the stamp of divine intervention?

Return to the case of the man who crosses a bridge one minute before it collapses. Let us alter the circumstances and suppose the man is driving on the bridge when the tragedy occurs. No one on the bridge survives, except for him. He is thrown from his car and lands unharmed in soft soil. Has a miracle occurred?

Given one meaning of the term, a miracle certainly has occurred, for a miracle may be understood as an unexpected, wonderful event, and the man's escape from injury is in that sense miraculous. But is the event miraculous in a stronger sense of the word—is the event an act of God that suspends laws of nature?

Some theists may be tempted to believe so, especially when several members of a local church come forward to say that as they were watching the events unfold, they saw a fiery chariot appear from the heavens, pick up the man as he was falling, and return him safely to earth. Do their reports increase the likelihood that a miracle occurred?

In a court of law, testimony is subject to cross-examination and may turn out to be mistaken. Assume, for instance, that two witnesses say that they observed the defendant Smith commit a robbery. Yet forty reliable others are prepared to testify that at the time in question Smith was playing baseball many miles away. Apparently, the two witnesses who thought they saw Smith commit the crime were mistaken. When challenged, though, the two insist they couldn't be wrong, certain they seemed to see Smith.

To assess their claim, we need to draw a distinction between statements such as "I see a star" and statements such as "I seem to see a star." If I see a star, then a star is present for me to see. I may be wrong that I am seeing a star, for perhaps I am seeing an airplane instead, but if I am right that I am seeing a star, the truth of my statement implies the existence of a star. If I only thought I was seeing a star but was actually seeing an airplane, I can still claim that I *seemed* to see a star. In making that claim sincerely, I am safe from error, but my saying that I seemed to see something doesn't imply the existence of what I seemed to see. In other words, statements such as "I see a star" may be false, but if they are true, they imply the existence of the thing perceived. Statements such as "I seem to see a star," if sincere, cannot be false but do not imply the existence of the thing seemingly perceived.

Confusion sets in if some persons claim that a thing exists because they seem to see it. What is necessary is that *if* they see something, it is present. What is also necessary is that if they *seem* to see something, they can't be wrong that they *seem* to see it; they can, however, be wrong that it is present.

In the case of the witnesses who seemed to see Smith commit the robbery, did they actually see what they thought they saw? To determine the reliability of a person's testimony, we assess it in light of questions such as the following: (1) How many witnesses saw the event? (2) Do the witnesses agree in all important respects? (3) Are they regarded as persons of reliable judgment? (4) Do they have any reason to want to see what they claim to have seen? (5) Is anyone, such as a magician, trying to mislead them? (6) Is their testimony incompatible with other evidence? (7) How likely is their testimony compared to the likelihood of any widely accepted views with which it is incompatible? (8) How plausible is an alternative explanation of why they seemed to see what they thought they saw?

In Smith's case, forty witnesses testify that they saw him playing baseball, whereas only two say they saw him commit the robbery. Let us presume that the testimony of the forty is in all important respects identical, that they are reliable persons with no reason to lie, that no one is trying to mislead them, that their testimony fits all the facts except for the accounts of the two dissenting witnesses, that the testimony of the forty is not incompatible with any laws of nature or other widely believed claims, and that Smith has an identical twin brother who doesn't play baseball but has previously been convicted of crimes and was known to be in the vicinity of the crime scene when the robbery occurred. Given all these factors, any reasonable jury would find Smith "not guilty."

Let us now use these same criteria to judge the plausibility of those who reported seeing a fiery chariot save the man falling from the bridge. Witnesses were few. We may suppose they each described the chariot somewhat differently, that their reliability may be suspect in view of their previous accounts of equally strange sightings, that their commitment to a particular type of theism may give them reason to wish to witness miracles, that they may be subject to the will of a leader who praises them for reporting supposed miracles, and that no traces of any chariot tracks are found in the ground where the man came to rest.

Most important, their reports imply the suspension of the law of gravity, a law as highly confirmed as any could be. Thus, the weight of the evidence suggests not that the law ceased to operate but that these observers made a mistake.

As to how they were misled, we might suppose that remains of a burning car found near where the man landed might have been thought to be a chariot. This hypothesis, while merely a guess, is nevertheless far more plausible than the possibility that the law of gravity was suspended while a fiery chariot appeared and disappeared.

I admit to having stacked the deck against those reporting the miracle by assuming weaknesses in their testimony that may not fit the facts in every case. Suppose, for instance, the witnesses were more numerous, independent, and reliable. Would such conditions increase the probability that a miracle occurred?

Not to a significant degree, for as Hume noted in his much-discussed account of miracles, "There must...be a uniform experience against every miraculous event, otherwise the event would not merit that appellation. And as a uniform experience amounts to a proof, there is here direct and full *proof* from the nature of the fact, against the existence of any miracle."[1]

In other words, because a miracle suspends a natural law, and because the evidence for the operation of such laws is overwhelming, the probability that a miracle occurred is always far less than the probability that the law continued to function. Thus, invariably any report of a miracle is highly unlikely.

Theists are most tempted to believe in a miracle when it involves the triumph of good over evil. If the man saved in the collapse of the bridge was of saintly character, whereas those killed in the accident were seeking to harm him, then considering the event miraculous is nearly irresistible. To assume, however, that God acts so that the good prosper while evildoers are punished is to agree with Job's friends, whom God rebuked for their mistaken views. After all, if we attribute wondrous events to God, who is responsible for horrendous ones?

---

1. David Hume, *An Enquiry Concerning Human Understanding* (New York: Oxford University Press, 1999), 173.

12

God Without Religion

THE ARGUMENT AGAINST BELIEVING in miracles also discourages accepting reports from those who claim to have directly experienced God and thereby learned God's will. Drawing on the distinction between statements like "I see a star" and "I seem to see a star," we need to distinguish between seeing God and only seeming to see God. Anyone may claim to have seemed to see God, and ordinarily we have no reason to doubt personal reports. Such testimony, however, is fallible; it does not prove that the person saw God. As Sidney Hook wrote, "Whether an actual angel speaks to me in my beatific vision or whether I only dreamed he spoke, the truth of what he says can only be tested in the same way I test what my neighbor says to me. For even my neighbor may claim to be a messenger of the Lord."[1]

Testimony of revelations, like testimony for miracles, needs to be examined in accord with standards of rationality. As in the previously discussed case of Smith, who was accused of robbery, the reports of witnesses should be assessed in the light of whether they all agree, whether they have any reason to want to experience what they claim to have experienced, whether their testimony is incompatible with other evidence, and so on.

1. Sidney Hook, *The Quest for Being* (New York: St. Martin's Press, 1961), 130–31.

Such tests, however, serve to undermine the credibility of those who report experiencing God and learning God's will. After all, as William L. Rowe observed, "These experiences are embedded in and support rival religious traditions that contradict one another...[T]hey can hardly all be veridical perceptions of a divine presence."[2] Bluntly put, Hindus don't report sensing the presence of Jesus and learning the divine message found in the New Testament. Furthermore, those who report experiences of God are apt to be seeking such revelations, and their claims often imply the implausible suspension of accepted laws of nature related to optics and acoustics.

Suppose these considerations convince you that, although God exists, no events, whether miracles or revelations, bear the unmistakable stamp of divine intervention. You might, therefore, subscribe to the account of theism that Hume in his *Dialogues Concerning Natural Religion* attributes to Philo the skeptic: "[T]he cause or causes of order in the universe probably bear some remote analogy to human intelligence."[3] Given, however, that anything probably bears some remote analogy to anything else, the implications of this position are indeterminate, resulting in Philo's observation that theism "affords no inference that affects human life."

Indeed, if we cannot understand God's ways, why be concerned about them? According to Epicurus, we may pray to the divine, but we have no reason to suppose that God is listening.[4]

A near contemporary of Epicurus, living far away, adopted a similar approach. Xunzi (pronounced "shun-see"), a Confucian scholar of the third century BCE, thought that ascribing to God a role in human events is misguided. "You pray for rain and it rains. Why? For no reason, I say. It is just as though you had not prayed for rain and it rained anyhow."[5] He views rites not as appeals to

2. William L. Rowe, *Philosophy of Religion: An Introduction*, Fourth Edition (Belmont, CA: Thomson/Wadsworth, 2007), 77.

3. *Dialogues Concerning Natural Religion*, 12: 33. Italics omitted.

4. *The Stoic and Epicurean Philosophers*, ed. Whitney J. Oates (New York: The Modern Library, 1940), 50.

5. Xunzi, *Basic Writings*, trans. Burton Watson (New York: Columbia University Press, 2003), 89.

otherworldly forces but as human inventions that ornament social life and serve as expressions of emotion.

Many centuries later in the West, deists held a similar position. They affirmed the existence of God but found formal religion superfluous and denied all claims to revelation, thus providing no reason to look to the divine as a source of help or hindrance. Among deists were Voltaire, Jean Jacques Rousseau, Benjamin Franklin, George Washington, and Thomas Jefferson, an estimable group indeed.

Thus, those who believe in God do not necessarily adhere to any religion. They are, in short, non-religious theists.

13

Playing the Odds

EVEN IF WE AGREE with those who deny insight into God's will, might prudence nevertheless dictate that we participate in an established theistic religion because each offers a well-trodden path relating to the divine? Even if these religions are not on the right track to truth, what has been lost by joining them and trying their ways?

This line of reasoning is similar to that offered by Blaise Pascal, who developed what has come to be known as Pascal's wager, an argument for why one should believe in God even without any proof of God's existence. Pascal argued that if you believe, and God exists, then you attain heavenly bliss; if you believe, and God doesn't exist, little is lost. On the other hand, if you don't believe, and God does exist, then you are doomed to the torments of damnation; if you don't believe, and God doesn't exist, little is gained. Thus, belief is the safest strategy.[1]

Pascal, however, failed to consider the possibility that a different kind of God might exist, for example, one who wishes us to hold only those beliefs supported by the available evidence. If such a God exists, then in the absence of evidence, not believing is the safest strategy.

---

1. See Blaise *Pascal, Pensees and Other Writings*, trans. Honor Levi (New York: Oxford University Press, 1995), 152–56.

A similar difficulty undermines the supposition that in the absence of knowledge about God, the safest strategy is to join a religion, pray to God, and hope for the best. After all, suppose God doesn't approve of any religions and doesn't wish to receive any prayers. What if God rewards those who shun such activities? In that case, not believing is the safest strategy.

Admittedly, this account of the divine nature is contrary to what many people suppose. They take as obvious that God wishes to receive our supplications and veneration, although why God wants them is unclear, especially because God is not supposed to have any needs. Leaving aside temporarily, however, the incomprehensibility of God, which would make it impossible for anyone to grasp God's nature, let me offer an analogy to suggest that what God wills may be contrary to widespread expectations.

Most children, although sadly not all, enter this world beloved by their parents who, having created them, make every effort to nurture and support them, sometimes even at great cost to the parents' own ambitions. In response, the children may dearly love one or both their parents, not merely honoring them in accord with the biblical injunction, but adoring them.

Yet sensible parents do not wish to be the object of their children's worship. To the contrary, they would find the situation distressing and believe that in some way they had failed as parents. Even though they welcome the love of an independent child who learns to make decisions and fulfill duties, parents do not seek nor would they want the single-minded devotion of a dependent child who relies on them to make all decisions and is unwilling to shoulder responsibilities.

If we are children of God, might not God, like a wise parent, wish those God created to be independent, not dependent? Might God disapprove of being worshipped at public services and prayed to at times of hardship? Might God instead favor those who meditated privately, if at all, performed good deeds rather than godly rituals, and displayed the fortitude to persevere in the face of difficulties without appealing for God's help? Perhaps, as Benjamin

Franklin wrote, "God helps them that help themselves."[2] Indeed, God's will may have been best understood by the prophet Amos when he attributed to God the following words:

> I loathe, I spurn your festivals,
> I am not appeased by your solemn assemblies,
> If you offer Me burnt offerings—or your meal offerings—
> I will not accept them;
> I will pay no heed
> To your gifts of fatlings.
> Spare Me the sound of your hymns,
> And let Me not hear the music of your lutes.
> But let justice well up like water,
> Righteousness like an unfailing stream.[3]

Thus, rather than venerating God and offering God supplications, we should focus our efforts on being considerate to others.

Granted, I have been speculating about matters that may lie beyond human understanding. If they do not, I believe my account of God's will is as plausible as another's. But if grasping the nature of the divine is impossible, then joining an established religion in an effort to find the truth is no more reasonable than not joining. In the absence of any relevant information, all bets are off.

---

2. *Franklin Writings*, ed. J. A. Leo Lemay (New York: Library of America, 1987), 1201.

3. Amos 5:21–24.

14

Why Worship God?

IN CHALLENGING THE APPROPRIATENESS of religious worship, I recognize that I am raising doubts about an activity many theists consider central to their relationship with God. After all, if we grant that the universe was created and is sustained by an omnipotent, omniscient, omni-benevolent God, why does God not deserve worship?

Note that simply praising God presents no problem, so long as, like the Psalmist, you believe, "The Heavens declare the glory of God, the sky proclaims His handiwork."[1] Of course, some, like Arthur Schopenhauer have been little impressed by our world, saying: "Unless *suffering is* the direct and immediate object of life, our existence must entirely fail of its aim."[2] Although the goodness of creation is thus open to dispute, praising God presents no conceptual difficulties.

How about displaying reverence for God? To revere someone is to regard that individual with profound respect. Thus, you might revere your mother or father, a beloved teacher, an inspiring

---

[1]. Psalms 19:2.

[2]. From "On the Sufferings of the World," in *The Will to Live: Selected Writings of Arthur Schopenhauer*, ed. Richard Taylor (Garden City, NY: Anchor Books, 1962), 215.

political leader, or a great artist. In that sense, you might also revere God, indeed, more than any other being.

But to worship is more than to revere, for in worshipping we deprecate ourselves and exalt another beyond challenge. Is worshipping in that sense ever appropriate?

To seek an answer, let us consider a hypothetical case. Suppose a fabulously wealthy developer decides to create a utopian town, providing all its inhabitants with a spacious home, a generous bank account, and the finest in schools, parks, roads, stores, and a variety of other amenities. Furthermore, this developer, a person of extraordinary wisdom and kindness, has planned to maintain the town far into the future. Presuming you reside in the town, what should be your attitude toward the developer?

No doubt you would admire the developer's planning and appreciate the developer's generosity. Probably you would support the community's expressing its gratitude to the developer by placing a statue in the town square, naming a building, or celebrating an annual holiday. The most appropriate option would to a large extent depend on what the developer prefers. As it happens, however, the developer answers no questions and is unavailable to anyone seeking direct interaction. Hence, none can be sure what the developer wishes.

How about worshipping the developer? Would that response make sense? Few, if any, would think so. But why the reluctance? After all, the developer has created and sustained the town, holds power over the town, has displayed extraordinary knowledge in planning the town, and acts as benevolently as possible toward the town's inhabitants. Why, then, would the town's inhabitants hesitate to worship the developer? An obvious reply is that the developer is not God. But how significant are the differences between them?

First, consider their powers. God is far more powerful than the developer, but the developer appears to possess all the power the town requires. Granted, the developer doesn't decide matters of life and death, but had the developer chosen to become the town's dictator, judging who is to live and who is to die, would exercising those powers render the developer more admirable? Quite the opposite. Furthermore, would the developer become more worthy of worship by creating more utopian towns? Even if doing so leads to greater acclaim, why would the developer become more worthy of worship by having created three, thirty, or hundreds of utopian towns?

Another difference between the developer and God relates to the scope of their respective knowledge. God knows everything that can be known,[3] while the developer doesn't, but the developer has near total knowledge of the town. If the developer acquired knowledge about more places, more people, and more things, would that increase in knowledge render the developer worthy of worship? Again, no. Suppose the developer was a master psychologist who understood the desires and fears of each person in the town. Would that knowledge increase the appropriateness of worshipping the developer? Hardly. After all, while the finest performers in a field of endeavor may deserve honors, even a perfect performance doesn't call for worshipping the performer.

The developer always acts ethically toward the town's inhabitants, while God always acts rightly in every situation. But does quantity of right acts matter? Most of us act rightly some times, some act rightly most times, and a few act rightly at all times. But even if the developer is in the latter category, worshipping the developer still appears inappropriate. Indeed, were an individual to seek to be an object of worship, that desire would itself suggest weakness, not strength, of character.

Which of God's attributes, if any, is supposed to imply that God deserves worship? God's power is overwhelming, but power alone does not call for worship. God's knowledge is as complete as possible, but immense learning, while admirable, does not imply the appropriateness of worship. God's goodness is perfect, but to be good is to be made uncomfortable by praise. God created and sustained the universe, but the developer's having created and

---

3. This formulation of the doctrine of God's omniscience is defended in my essay, "Does God Know the Future?" in Steven M. Cahn, *A Philosopher's Journey: Essays from Six Decades* (Eugene, OR: Wipf and Stock Publishers, 2020), 33–37.

sustained the town (or innumerable such towns) does not suggest that the developer should be worshipped. Why is God different? While each attribute of God taken alone does not justify the worship of God, perhaps all together do. I see no argument, however, why possessing any combination of attributes renders God more worthy of worship than does each attribute separately.

What, then, should be the appropriate attitude toward God? The best answer I know is implicit in chapter 18 of the Book of Genesis, in which God tells Abraham that God is considering destroying the cities of Sodom and Gomorrah. Here is the key passage:

> Abraham came forward and said, "Will You sweep away the innocent along with the guilty? What if there should be fifty innocent within the city, will You then wipe out the place and not forgive it for the sake of the innocent who are in it? Far be it from You to do such a thing, to bring death upon the innocent as well as the guilty, so that innocent and guilty fare alike. Far be it from You! Shall not the Judge of all the earth deal justly? And the Lord answered, "If I find within the city of Sodom fifty innocent ones, I will forgive the whole place for their sake." Abraham spoke up, saying, "Here I venture to speak to my Lord, I who am but dust and ashes: What if the fifty innocent should lack five? Will You destroy the whole city for want of the five? And He answered, "I will not destroy if I find forty-five there." But he spoke to Him again, and said, "What if forty should be found there?" And He answered, "I will not do it, for the sake of the forty." And he said, "Let not my Lord be angry if I go on: What if thirty should be found there?" And He answered, "I will not do it if I find thirty there." And he said, "I venture again to speak to my Lord: What if twenty should be found there?" And He answered, "I will not destroy, for the sake of the twenty." And he said, "Let not my Lord be angry if I speak but this last time. What if ten should be found there?" And He answered, "I will not destroy, for the sake of the ten."[4]

---

4. Genesis 18:23–32.

While the story, four chapters later, of God's commanding Abraham to prepare the sacrifice of his son Isaac, has attracted far more attention than the story of Abraham bargaining with God, I find the earlier story more revelatory about the appropriate relationship between human beings and God.

To begin with, Abraham recognizes his own cosmic insignificance as compared to God. Nevertheless, Abraham challenges the justice of God's plan to destroy Sodom. Hence, the story is inconsistent with the divine command theory of morality, according to which justice is defined by whatever God commands. Abraham asks God to reflect on the justice of destroying Sodom, should the city contain fifty innocents. If the goodness of an action were determined by God's will, then God's plan to destroy Sodom could not be shown to be wrong, for whatever God commanded would be right. By appealing to God's wish to act justly, however, Abraham convinces God to act differently because God's proposed action would not be just. But then the concept of justice is not merely a matter of God's will but an independent standard that God recognizes. If the supposed reason to worship God is that God's will creates morality, then that consideration does not serve as a justification for worshipping God because although God always acts in accordance with morality, God does not create it.

Note that while Abraham recognizes his powers are no match for God's, God is subject to the power of reason. Abraham could not have prevented God from destroying Sodom, but Abraham uses the power inherent in sound reasoning to change the will of God. Thus, humanity is not without leverage against God, and if the reason to worship God is presumed to be that God has all power and humanity has none, the story of Abraham's bargaining with God indicates that such a justification is mistaken.

Notice that God is subject to change. God begins by planning to destroy Sodom but then agrees to condition that decision on whether the city might contain innocent people, whether fifty, forty-five, forty, thirty, twenty, or ten. For those who worship God because God is thought to be unchanging, that justification is ineffective because God keeps changing the number of innocent persons required to save Sodom from destruction.

Still, God might be thought worthy of worship because of God's controlling whether we live or die. In the chilling words of Puritan minister, theologian, and philosopher Jonathan Edwards,

> The God that holds you over the pit of Hell, much as one holds a spider, or some loathsome insect, over the fire, abhors you, and is dreadfully provoked; his wrath towards you burns like fire; he looks upon you as worthy of nothing else, but to be cast into the fire; he is of purer eyes than to bear to have you in his sight; you are ten thousand times so abominable in in his eyes as the most hateful venomous serpent is in ours. You have offended him infinitely more than ever a stubborn rebel did his prince; and yet 'tis nothing but his hand that holds you from falling into that fire every moment.

No wonder Edwards was unable to finish his sermon as "there was a great moaning and crying out throughout the whole house...The tumult only increased as the shrieks and cries were piercing and amazing."[5] In short, Edwards forced the congregation to confront the awful truth that they were doomed, and only God could save them.

Surely God, as described by Edwards, is terrifying. If you make a wrong move with God, you will be condemned to a horrendous fate. No wonder religious services often call for bowing one's head, averting one's eyes, kneeling, and even groveling. In the spirit of humbling oneself, rituals are performed and prayers recited as exactly as possible so not to anger God. The prevalent emotion is fear, along with the hope that we and our loved ones will be spared God's wrath.

The obvious analogy is between God and a despot. In the despot's country, inhabitants take great pains to avoid engaging in any actions that would call attention to themselves and attract the despot's anger. Obviously, however, no despot should be worshipped,

---

5. The quoted material is found in George M. Marsden, *Jonathan Edwards: A Life* (New Haven and London: Yale University Press, 2003,), 220, 223.

although inhabitants may be forced to go through the motions of appearing to worship the despot.

Of course, the despot, unlike God, is hardly benevolent and surely not omni-benevolent. The goodness of God, however, is not a reason to worship God but, on the contrary, a reason *not* to worship God, because a good being would not want to be worshipped. And that insight is exemplified in the story of Abraham bargaining with God about the destruction of Sodom.

When Abraham suggests to God that God needs to think further about the action God is about to take, God does not disregard Abraham, or berate him, or tell him that he has no right to be raising doubts. Rather, God listens to Abraham's reasoning and makes a suitable adjustment to the plan as originally proposed. Had Abraham worshipped God, then Abraham would simply have accepted God's plan, praising it and extolling God. To worship is to venerate or pay homage, not to question and challenge.

Rabbi Mordecai M. Kaplan, founder of Reconstructionist Judaism (now Reconstructing Judaism), which explicitly rejects supernaturalism, was once a guest speaker at a religious service where the congregation recited the proverb "Trust in the Lord with all your heart. And do not rely on your own understanding."[6] Rabbi Kaplan announced to the assemblage that this prayer was one he refused to utter because he could not relinquish the right to trust his own powers of reason. His attitude is an echo of Abraham's bargaining with God, for Abraham did not trust God's judgment about Sodom. Instead, Abraham relied on his own understanding and successfully challenged God's plan.

I would propose that those who believe in God should follow the example of Abraham, praising God as frequently and fervently as wished, acclaiming God's omnipotence, omniscience, and omni-benevolence, and thanking God profusely for creating and sustaining the universe. Like Abraham, though, believers should not treat the word of God as beyond challenge by human reason. God may be worthy of as much praise and gratitude as human beings can offer, but even God is not to be worshipped.

6. Proverbs 3:5.

15

Religions

TO THIS POINT, I have treated the decision to join a religion as if the choice among religions does not matter. The divergences among them, however, are vast, including different rituals, different prayers, different metaphysical systems, and different moral beliefs.

Judaism believes in a unitary god, Zoroastrianism in two gods, Christianity in a triune god, and Shinto in gods or spirits too numerous to count; Theravada Buddhism, Samkhya Hinduism, and Mimamsa Hinduism believe in no gods at all. The Confucian Mencius teaches that human nature is essentially good; Christians view human nature as tainted by original sin. Hindus consider the soul immortal; Buddhists view it as impermanent. Muslims practice *purdah*, the seclusion of women; in Shinto, female priests conduct religious ceremonies. The Sikh religion is unique in requiring its members to have uncut hair, a bracelet, a dagger, a comb, and shorts as an undergarment.

Indeed, every belief and practice of any particular religion is rejected by some other religion. Furthermore, although almost every religion has its own holy writings thought to embody the truth as revealed to inspired prophets, interpretations of scripture differ in each religion and have frequently given rise to fierce internal doctrinal disputes. Recall that despite the many matters about which

Protestants and Catholics agree, their disagreements led to centuries of bloodshed.

Such differences cannot be overcome by embracing all religions as variations on a single theme because religions are typically exclusive: accepting one implies not accepting others. We may respect a religion or admire aspects of it, but to accept it fully requires conversion, for each religion claims to be correct in belief and practice, and these claims are in conflict. But what arguments can establish the truth of one religion and the falsity of all others?

As a test case, consider Jainism, an ancient faith from India. It denies a creator God and is thus atheistic. Through self-mortification, its adherents seek to transcend the world and achieve a peace beyond all concerns. The central virtue is nonviolence against any living being. To this end, all adherents must be vegetarians and cannot serve as butchers or soldiers. Its monks wear a gauze mask over the mouth to prevent the unintentional inhalation of an innocent insect. They are also required to sweep the ground in front of them as they walk so as not to crush anything alive. They renounce all worldly attachments as well as any sensual pleasures, and they vow not to eat after sunset. If psychologically strong enough to achieve the goal of neglecting every personal interest, the monks commit suicide by self-starvation, thereby ridding the soul of all passions and bringing an appropriate close to an ethical life. The two main sects are divided over the question of whether the monks, to symbolize their complete renunciation of the material world, should practice nudity.

Can any argument demonstrate why Christianity, for example, is superior to Jainism? Granted, any one of their differing metaphysical or ethical principles could be isolated and subjected to critical scrutiny. In view of their disagreements about so many fundamental matters, though, how could advocates for the two religions profitably discuss their opposing outlooks and practices, and how could their disagreements be rationally resolved?

Note that an appeal to numbers would not settle the issue. Worldwide, Christianity has nearly 500 times as many adherents as Jainism, but Buddhism, Hinduism, and Islam together have hundreds of millions more adherents than Christianity. Whatever may be the relevance of such statistics to a sociologist of religion, they bear no philosophical significance. After all, at one time most people thought the sun went around the earth; nevertheless, this opinion was false.

Some Christians might argue that the beliefs and practices of Jainism are too strange to be taken seriously. But how would the beliefs and practices of Christianity appear to Jains? What would they think of the immaculate conception, virgin birth, transubstantiation, and resurrection? What would they think of using a Roman device of torture as a central religious symbol? What would they think of the claim that the moral lapses of a person living today are forgiven because approximately two thousand years ago the son of God in the person of a Jewish teacher was put to death?

Each religion reflects the culture in which it develops, and cultures are not true or false, provable or disprovable, although one may be richer in some respects than another. Yet a culture is not tested by arguments, nor are religions. They are less like scientific theories and more like works of art, not adding to our factual knowledge but enabling many to enrich their response to the challenges of the human condition.

Some have said that religions, regardless of the chasms between them, have been a force for good in human history. Hume, on the other hand, a leading historian as well as philosopher, forcefully expressed the opposite view of religion: "Factions, civil wars, persecutions, subversions of government, oppression, slavery; these are the dismal consequences which always attend its prevalence over the minds of men. If the religious spirit be ever mentioned in any historical narration, we are sure to meet afterwards with a detail of the miseries which attend it."[1]

Surely, the record of religion is mixed: Sublime ideals and saintly acts are balanced by ignoble sentiments and horrendous practices. Religion as such is neither good nor evil. Religions have been both.

1. Hume, 12, 11.

16

Religion Without God

WHILE RECOGNIZING THE MULTIPLICITY of religions, we nevertheless are inclined to suppose that all are akin to the one we happen to know best. For example, many Christians believe that all religions place heavy emphasis on an afterlife, although the central concern of Judaism is life in this world, not the next. Similarly, many Christians and Jews suppose that to be religious requires belief in a supernatural God. Even when told of exceptions to this rule, they suspect that a religion without supernaturalism is somehow incoherent.

I propose to show that nothing in the theory or practice of religion—not ritual, not prayer, not metaphysical belief, not moral commitment—necessitates a commitment to theism. In other words, just as one may be a nonreligious theist, so one can be a religious agnostic or atheist.

Consider first the concept of a ritual, a prescribed symbolic action. In the case of religion, the ritual is prescribed by a religious organization, and the act symbolizes some aspect of religious belief. If the religion is supernaturalistic (that is, if it believes in a supernatural deity or deities), then those who reject such theology may as a result consider any ritual irrational. Yet, although particular rituals may be based on irrational beliefs, nothing about the practice of ritual is inherently irrational.

Think of two people shaking hands when meeting. This act is a ritual, prescribed by our society and symbolic of the individuals' mutual respect. The act is in no way irrational. If people shook hands in order to ward off evil demons, then shaking hands would indeed be irrational. That reason, however, is not why people shake hands. The ritual may have originated as a gesture of peace indicating that the proffered hand is without a weapon. Regardless, the ritual has no connection with God or demons but now indicates the respectful attitude one person has toward another.

Some might assume that the ritual of handshaking escapes irrationality only because the ritual is not prescribed by any specific organization and is not part of an elaborate ceremony. To see that this assumption is false, consider the graduation ceremony at a college. The graduates and faculty members all wear peculiar hats and robes, and the participants stand and sit at appropriate times. The ceremony, however, is not at all irrational. Indeed, the rites of graduation day, far from being irrational, are symbolic of commitment to the process of education and the life of reason.

At first glance, rituals may seem a comparatively insignificant feature of life, yet they are a pervasive and treasured aspect of human experience. Who would want to eliminate the customs associated with holidays such as Memorial Day or Thanksgiving? What would college football be without songs, cheers, flags, and the innumerable other symbolic features surrounding the game? Those who disdain popular rituals typically proceed to establish their own distinctive ones, such as characteristic habits of dress, symbolizing a rejection of traditional mores.

Religious persons, like all others, search for appropriate means of emphasizing their commitment to a group or its values. Rituals serve this purpose. Granted, supernaturalistic religion has often fused its rituals with superstition, but nonreligious rituals can be equally superstitious. For instance, most Americans view the Fourth of July as an occasion on which they can express pride in their country's heritage. With this purpose in mind, the holiday is one of great significance. If, however, the singing of the fourth verse of "The Star-Spangled Banner" four times on the Fourth of

July were thought to protect our country against future disasters, then the original meaning of the holiday would be lost in a maze of superstition.

A naturalistic (that is, non-supernaturalistic) religion need not utilize ritual in a superstitious manner, because such a religion does not employ rituals to please a benevolent deity or appease an angry one. Rather, naturalistic religion views rituals, in the words of Rabbi Jack J. Cohen, as "the enhancement of life through the dramatization of great ideals."[1] If a group places great stress on justice or freedom, why should the group not utilize ritual to emphasize these goals? Such a use of ritual serves to solidify the group and strengthen its devotion to its expressed purposes. These are buttressed if the ritual in question has the force of tradition, having been performed by many generations who have belonged to the same group and struggled to achieve the same goals. Ritual so conceived is not a form of superstition but a reasonable means of strengthening religious commitment, as useful to naturalistic as to supernaturalistic religion.

Let us next turn to the concept of prayer. Some might suppose that naturalistic religion could have no use for prayer as its proponents do not believe in the existence of the supernatural being to whom it is addressed. This objection oversimplifies the concept of prayer, focusing attention on one type while neglecting an equally important but different sort.

Supernaturalistic religion makes extensive use of petitionary prayer, which asks a supernatural being for favors. These may range from the personal happiness of the petitioner to the general welfare of all society. Because petitionary prayer rests on the assumption that a supernatural being exists, such prayer clearly has no place in a naturalistic religion.

Not all prayers, however, are prayers of petition. Prayers of meditation, for example, do not request favors of supernatural. beings. Rather, these prayers provide the opportunity for persons to rethink their fundamental commitments and rededicate themselves to their ideals. Such prayers may take the form of silent

1. Jack J. Cohen, 50.

devotion or involve oral repetition of central texts. Just as Americans repeat the Pledge of Allegiance and reread the Gettysburg Address, so adherents of naturalistic religion repeat the statements of their ideals and reread the documents that embody their traditional beliefs.

Granted, supernaturalistic religions, to the extent that they utilize prayers of meditation, tend to treat them irrationally by supposing that to be of value they need to be uttered a precise number of times under certain specific conditions. Yet prayer need not be viewed in this way. Rather, as Sir Julian Huxley wrote, prayer "permits the bringing before the mind of a world of thought which in most people must inevitably be absent during the occupation of ordinary life...[I]t is the means by which the mind may fix itself upon this or that noble or beautiful or awe-inspiring idea, and so grow to it and come to realize it more fully."[2]

This use of prayer may be enhanced by song, instrumental music, and various types of symbolism. These elements fused together provide the means for adherents of naturalistic religion to engage in religious services akin to those engaged in by adherents of supernaturalistic religion. The difference between the two services is that participants in the latter come to relate to God, whereas participants in the former come to relate to their fellow human beings and the world in which we live.

Thus far we have examined how ritual and prayer can be utilized in naturalistic religion, but adopting a religious perspectives also involves metaphysical beliefs and moral commitments. Can these be maintained without recourse to supernaturalism?

If we use them term *metaphysics* in its usual sense, referring to the systematic study of the most basic features of existence, then a metaphysical system may be either supernaturalistic or naturalistic. Representative of a supernaturalistic theory are René Descartes and Gottfried Leibniz. Representative of a naturalistic theory are Baruch Spinoza and John Dewey.

---

2. Julian Huxley, *Religion Without Revelation* (New York: New American Library, 1957), 141.

Spinoza's *Ethics*, for example, one of the greatest of metaphysical works, explicitly rejects the view that any being exists apart from Nature itself. Identifying God with Nature as a whole, Spinoza stresses that the good life consists in understanding Nature. In his words, "[O]ur salvation, or blessedness, or freedom consists in a constant and eternal love toward God."[3] Spinoza's concept of God is explicitly not supernaturalistic, and Spinoza's metaphysical system thus exemplifies not only a naturalistic metaphysics but also the possibility of reinterpreting the concept of God within a naturalistic framework.

Can those who do not believe in a supernaturalistic God commit themselves to moral principles, or is the acceptance of moral principles dependent on the acceptance of supernaturalism? Some have assumed that those who reject a supernaturalistic God are necessarily immoral, for their denial of the existence of God leaves them free to act without fear of divine punishment. This assumption, however, is seriously mistaken.

The refutation of the view that morality must rest on belief in a supernatural God was provided more than two thousand years ago in Plato's remarkable dialogue *Euthyphro*. There Socrates asks the overconfident Euthyphro whether actions are right because God says they are right, or whether God says actions are right because they are right.

In other words, Socrates is inquiring whether actions are right because of God's fiat or whether God is subject to moral standards. If actions are right because of God's command, then anything God commands would be right. Had God commanded adultery, stealing, and murder, then adultery, stealing, and murder would be right—surely an unsettling and to most an unacceptable conclusion.

Granted, some may be willing to adopt this discomforting view, but then they face another difficulty. If the good is whatever God commands, to say that God's commands are good amounts to saying that God's commands are God's commands, a mere

---

3. Baruch Spinoza, *Ethics*, ed. James Gutmann (New York: Hafner, 1957), pt. V, prop. 36, note.

tautology. In that case, the possibility of meaningfully praising the goodness of God would be lost.

The lesson here is that might does not make right, even if the might is the infinite might of God. To act morally is neither to act out of fear of punishment nor to act as one is commanded. Rather, it is to act as one ought to act, and how one ought to act is not dependent on anyone's power, even if the power is divine.

Thus, actions are not right because God commands them; on the contrary, God commands them because they are right. What is right is independent of what God commands, for to be right, what God commands must conform to an independent standard. Recall that in the story of Abraham's bargaining with God, Abraham appeals to such an independent standard whose appropriateness God recognizes.

We could act intentionally in accord with a moral standard without believing in the existence of God; therefore, morality does not rest on that belief. Consequently, those who do not believe in God can be highly moral (as well as immoral) people, and those who do believe in the existence of God can be highly immoral (as well as moral) people. This conclusion should come as no surprise to anyone who has contrasted the benevolent life of the Buddha, the inspiring teacher and atheist, with the malevolent life of the monk Tomás de Torquemada, who devised and enforced the boundless cruelties of the Spanish Inquisition.

We have now seen that naturalistic religion is a genuine possibility because reasonable individuals may perform rituals, utter prayers, accept metaphysical beliefs, and commit themselves to moral principles without believing in supernaturalism. Indeed, even a supernaturalistic religion such as Judaism or Christianity may be reinterpreted to eliminate any commitment to supernaturalism.

Here, for example, is how Rabbi Mordecai M. Kaplan, an opponent of supernaturalism, responded to a skeptic who asked why, if the Bible isn't taken literally, Jews should nevertheless observe the Sabbath:

> We observe the Sabbath not so much because of the account of its origin in Genesis, as because of the role it

has come to play in the spiritual life of our People and of mankind. . . .The Sabbath day sanctifies our life by what it contributes to making us truly human and helping us to transcend those instincts and passions that are part of our heritage from the sub-human.[4]

And here is an account of the Holy Communion from one of the major figures in the Christian "Death of God" movement, the Anglican Bishop of Woolwich John A. T. Robinson, who denied the existence of a God "up there" or "out there":

> Too often. . . .it ceases to be the holy meal, and becomes a religious service in which we turn our backs on the common and the community and in individualistic devotion go to 'make our communion' with 'the God out there.' This is the essence of the religious perversion, when worship becomes a realm into which to withdraw from the world to 'be with God'—even if it is only in order to receive strength to go back into it. In this case the entire realm of the non-religious (in other words, 'life') is relegated to the profane.[5]

Furthermore, a naturalistic religion can also be developed without deriving it from a supernatural religion. Consider, for example, the outlook of Charles Frankel, another opponent of supernaturalism, who nevertheless believed that religion, shorn of irrationality, can make a distinctive contribution to human life, providing deliverance from vanity, triumph over meanness, and endurance in the face of tragedy:"[I] seems to me not impossible that a religion could draw the genuine and passionate adherence of its members while it claimed nothing more than to be poetry in which men might participate and from which they might draw strength and light."[6]

---

4. Mordecai M. Kaplan, *Judaism Without Supernaturalism* (New York: The Reconstructionist Press, 1958), 115–16.

5. John A. T. Robinson, *Honest to God* (Philadelphia: The Westminster Press, 1963), 86–87.

6. Charles Frankel, *The Love of Anxiety and Other Essays* (New York, Evanston, and London: Harper & Row Publishers, 1965), 192.

Such naturalistic options are philosophically respectable. Whether to choose any of them is for each person to decide.

17

Heaven

FOR MANY THEISTS, A strong reason to reject naturalism and instead accept supernaturalism is its offering the "sure and certain hope of resurrection to eternal life."[1] After all, how important would God's existence be if it did not include the possibility of a blissful afterlife in which good people abide forever in a place of joy? Yet the concept of heaven raises numerous conceptual problems.

To begin, where is heaven? Those who speak of it often look upward, but would travel to Mars, Jupiter, or the nearest galaxy bring us closer to heaven? Or is heaven not in space? Might it have no location? If people go to heaven, they go somewhere. But to where do they journey, how long does the trip take, and what might they experience on the way? No one knows.

When we die, our bodies stop functioning and may even be destroyed. What form will they take in heaven? Will they look as they did when we were ten, forty, or seventy? If a person suffered from diabetes, will the resurrected body suffer from the disease? Indeed, if a person was ill for decades, will the resurrected body suddenly enjoy health that was rarely, if ever, attained in life? No one knows.

---

1. *The Books off Common Prayer* (New York: Penguin Books, 2012), 338.

If a new body is provided, would the resurrected person be identical to the person who died? If a ship is destroyed and an identical one built, the second is different from the first. Similarly, if a person is destroyed and an identical one created, the second is different from the first. In that case, the original person would be lost.

A way to avoid difficulties about resurrected bodies is to suppose that after death, survivors are not bodies but souls. Yet what is a soul? Supposedly, when added to a body, a soul converts it into a person. Of course, if the soul itself can think and feel, it is a person without a body. How, then, does it become a person when it enters a body? Can two souls inhabit a single body, or is the arrangement only one soul per person? Do non-human animals have souls? How would we know?

A crucial question concerns the personality of the resurrected person. Suppose Jones is charitable, loyal, and humorous, and enjoys gardening, listening to classical music, playing tennis, and taking trips with friends. After death, will the resurrected Jones have the same character and interests? If not, in what sense is the resurrected person appropriately identified as Jones?

To see an even greater difficulty, consider two acquaintances, Peters and Peterson. Peters looks forward to spending eternity with Peterson, whereas Peterson looks forward to being forever free of Peters. Assuming they retain their fundamental likes and dislikes, how can they both attain heavenly bliss?

Other problems arise when we try to understand the relationship between those in heaven and those on earth. The common supposition is that those whose die maintain an interest in events of this world. For example, a loving father who taught his daughter to become a championship swimmer will presumably after his death take pride if his daughter wins an Olympic medal. But that supposition, while perhaps comforting to the daughter, turns those in heaven into spectators of the living, watching intently as events unfold. What, then, becomes of heavenly bliss? How can heaven bring peaceful existence if the triumphs and tragedies of this world remain the focus of attention?

If those in heaven are unconcerned about events on earth, however, the relationship between those alive and those dead is broken. After all, if the father of the swimming champion no longer cares whether his daughter succeeds athletically or otherwise, in what sense is he still her loving father?

A further question is what we will find in heaven. Consider the case of Willie Mays, the spectacular baseball player whose greatest joy was to play the game he loved. Presumably bats, balls, and gloves are not found there, so what does Willie Mays do? Assuming he is the same person who made that spectacular catch in the 1954 World Series, how can the pleasures that supposedly await him in heaven match those he knew on earth?

One answer is that worldly delights pale in comparison with the delights of experiencing God. But how long can we find ecstasy in sheer contemplation, even if the object of our attention is divine? In the absence of events, even the most passionate love grows dull. Eventually we want to do something with or for those we love, not just remain endlessly in their presence.

In addition, why assume everyone will find delight in the presence of the divine? If someone was cantankerous in life, does that person remain cantankerous in heaven? If so, what becomes of eternal bliss? If not, what becomes of the individual's distinctive personality?

Even granting these numerous difficulties, the hope for heaven is understandable. After all, death looms for all. Like boaters riding long rapids heading inexorably toward a deadly waterfall, we can take pleasure in the passing scene so long as we don't focus on our destination. What we cannot do is stop the current or change its direction, for we are caught in the grip of time. Yet heaven offers us an escape. There we can live forever, surrounded by those for whom we care and safe in the eternal home, abiding in the light and goodness of God.

The vision is compelling. But given all the bewildering questions that beset any attempt to provide a persuasive or even coherent account of survival in a next world, I conclude that speculation about such obscure matters does not provide a reasonable foundation for belief in supernaturalism.[2]

---

2. I shall not dwell on the concept of hell, infinite punishment for finite wickedness, because it raises not only as many perplexing metaphysical issues as the concept of heaven but also additional moral ones. These are persuasively presented by Marilyn McCord Adams in "The Problem of Hell: A Problem of Evil for Christians," in *Reasoned Faith, Essays in Philosophical Theology in Honor of Norman Kretzmann*, ed. Eleonore Stump (Ithaca: Cornell University Press, 1993), 301–27. The late author, a professor of philosophy at UCLA, Yale, Rutgers, and other universities, was also an ordained priest in the Episcopal Church and Canon Emeritus at Christ Church Cathedral, Oxford. She concluded that damnation is a horror that exceeds our conceptual powers and should be rejected in favor of a doctrine of universal salvation. Thus, she returned the focus to heaven.

18

Life Without God

AN ASSUMPTION COMMON TO many theists is that if God doesn't exist, our lives are somehow diminished. Why accept this view? In any case, we are still alive as are others we cherish. We still experience times of health and sickness, We still strive to achieve goals, We still relish successes and regret failures, We still witness inspiring acts of goodness and disheartening deeds of evil. We still face moral problems and make difficult decisions.

Granted, we cannot expect help from God. Yet even if God exists, our choices are our own, not God's. We cannot rest secure in the belief that God is taking care of us, for as we have seen, the existence of God is consistent with the occurrence of all manner of tragedy.

Would life without God lack meaning? The answer depends on what sort of meaning a life can have. If a meaningful life is taken to be one in which each individual plays a role in a divine drama, entering and exiting the stage at an appointed time to serve God's purposes, then in the absence of God, life has no meaning.

Why assume, however, that people cannot have their own purposes, independent of any divine playwright? Suppose I wish to devote my life to teaching philosophy, you wish to devote your life to providing medical care to the sick, and others wish to devote their lives to composing music, cultivating a garden, or raising a family. Why aren't these activities meaningful? None of them depends on the existence of God. They nevertheless provide life with significance. They are freely chosen, not preordained, but so much the better. They are expressions of our own personalities and values.

Or is the problem supposed to be that in the absence of God, we are unable to decide which values or moral principles to accept? This challenge can be met by using reason to assess specific ethical judgments in the light of shared human concerns and our common experience.

To illustrate the process, let us consider in turn various moral principles that have been thought by many to embody the will of God but that, regardless of whether God exists, fall short of providing an entirely satisfactory foundation for morality. These rules, whatever their origin, are not immune from difficulties that can be recognized by theists and non-theists alike.

Consider the Golden Rule, a principle endorsed by various religious traditions. Its positive formulation is attributed to Jesus: "In everything do to others as you would have them do to you."[1] The negative formulation, which appeared at least five centuries earlier, is attributed to Confucius and was proposed about two millennia ago by the Jewish sage Hillel: "What is hateful to you, do not to your neighbor."[2] Is either of these versions entirely acceptable?

Examine first the positive formulation. Granted, we usually should treat others as we would wish them to treat us. For instance, we should go to the aid of an injured person, just as we would wish that person to come to our aid if we were injured. If we always followed this rule, however, the results would be unfortunate. Masochists, for instance, derive pleasure from being hurt. Were they to act according to the principle in question, their duty would be to inflict pain, thereby doing to others as they wish done to themselves. Similarly, consider a person who enjoys receiving telephone calls, regardless of who is calling. The principle would require that person to telephone everyone, thereby reciprocating preferred treatment. Indeed, strictly speaking, to fulfill the positive

1. Matthew 7:12.
2. *The Babylonian Talmud* (London: Soncino Press, 1938), Shabbath, 31a.

formulation of the Golden Rule would be impossible because we wish so many to do so much for us that we would not have time to do all that is necessary to treat them likewise. As Walter Kaufman commented, "Anyone who tried to live up to Jesus' rule would become an insufferable nuisance."[3]

In this respect, the negative formulation of the Golden Rule is preferable because it does not imply innumerable duties toward everyone else. Neither does it imply that masochists ought to inflict pain on others, nor that those who enjoy receiving telephone calls ought themselves to make calls. While the negative formulation does not require these actions, neither does it forbid them. It enjoins us not to do to others what is hateful to ourselves, but pain is not hateful to the masochist and innumerable calls are not hateful to the telephone enthusiast. Thus, the negative formulation, though superior in one way to the positive formulation, is not without weakness. It does not prohibit actions that ought to be prohibited.

Whether the Golden Rule in either formulation is supposed to be of divine origin makes no difference in our assessment. All can agree that, whatever its source, the principle does not by itself serve as the ultimate moral touchstone.

Even the Ten Commandments, accepted by a variety of religions, also have their limitations. Consider the Second Commandment, which, after prohibiting the making or serving of sculptured images, goes on to say: "For I the Lord your God am an impassioned God, visiting the guilt of the parents upon the children, upon the third and upon the fourth generations of those who reject Me, but showing kindness to the thousandth generation of those who love Me and keep My commandments."[4] But to punish one person for the moral lapses of another is unethical, as is rewarding a person for the good deeds of another. This point was made emphatically by the prophet Ezekiel, who declared: "A child shall not share the burden of a parent's guilt, nor shall a parent share the

---

3. Walter Kaufman, *The Faith of a Heretic* (New York: Doubleday, 1963), 212.

4. Exodus 20:5–6.

burden of a child's guilt; the righteousness of the righteous shall be accounted to him alone."[5] Incidentally, Ezekiel's principles rule out the possibility that anyone, including God, could absolve us of responsibility for our failings. If we act immorally, we cannot avoid the blame.[6]

The Fifth Commandment instructs individuals to honor their father and mother. Suppose, however, parents break the Second Commandment by making and worshipping sculptured images. Or perhaps they break some of the remaining commandments by coveting a neighbor's property, bearing false witness, stealing, engaging in adultery, or even committing murder. Although they might still merit their child's concern, parents who acted in such ways would not deserve to be honored.

Two of the commandments take slavery for granted. The Fourth, which requires individuals to remember the Sabbath day and keep it holy, prohibits work at that time by "you, your son or daughter, your male or female slave."[7] The Tenth prohibits coveting anything that belongs to a neighbor, including his "wife, or his male or female slave."[8] Slavery we all now agree is unethical, yet the Ten Commandments treat it as an acceptable practice.

A further problem is that the Commandments are stated as if they allow no exceptions. Yet under certain circumstances, not to break a Commandment would be widely regarded as immoral. For example, if a young girl's life depended on her mother's stealing a small amount of money from a wealthy, immoral person, most would view the theft favorably.

---

5. Ezekial 18:20.
6. While the power to forgive is often ascribed to God, the late Canadian philosopher Anne C. Mines, who taught at the University of Waterloo, ably defended the view that the divine attributes, such as perfection and omniscience, are inconsistent with God's reversing a judgment and forgiving wrongdoers. See her article "God and Omniscience," *The Philosophical Quarterly*, 25 (1975), 138–150, reprinted in *Contemporary Philosophy of Religion*, eds. Steven M. Cahn and David Shatz (New York: Oxford University Press, 1982), 32–45.
7. Exodus 21:10.
8. Exodus 20:14.

Not only do certain circumstances call for making exceptions to the Commandments, but situations can develop in which fulfilling one Commandment would amount to breaking another. If, for instance, a man had to work on the Sabbath in order to take his critically ill father to the hospital, the Commandment to honor one's father and mother would take precedence over the Commandment not to work on the Sabbath. The Commandments require exceptions but do not themselves provide any guidance for when or how. Thus, regardless of claims of their divine origin and despite their moral worth, the Ten Commandments fall short as an ultimate guide to morality.

The same is true of the sacred Christian text, the Sermon on the Mount. Amid its beauties of language and thought, we find such an unacceptable principles as "[I]f your right hand cause you to sin, cut it off and throw it away."[9] Any statement, of course, can be interpreted to render it sensible, but taken literally, thieves cutting off their hands would be acts of lunacy. If, however, the statement is not to be taken literally, it provides an ambiguous guide to moral action.

A similar problem is implicit in Jesus's instruction that "whoever marries a divorced woman commits adultery."[10] Few would find such a principle morally acceptable. What of Jesus's saying, "[D]o not worry about your life, what you will eat or what you will drink."[11] Wouldn't such a lack of concern for oneself be a sign of a psychological problem as well as an unfair drain on family and friends?

If these sayings appear peripheral to Jesus's principal message, consider this central passage: "Do not resist an evildoer. But if anyone strikes you on the right side, turn the other also; and if anyone wants to sue you and take your coat, give your cloak as well."[12] The difficulty with this approach is that in order to avoid the triumph of evil, those who adhere to pacifism depend on others' not adhering to it. For that reason, throughout history many

9. Matthew 5:30.
10. Matthew 5:32.
11. Matthew 6:25.
12. Matthew 5:39.

who have considered themselves devout Christians have on occasion put aside the Sermon on the Mount and picked up their weapons. Indeed, when Jesus entered Jerusalem, he "drove out all who were selling and buying in the temple and he overturned the tables of the money changers and the seats of those who sold doves."[13] So much for turning the other cheek.

Over centuries, many have found the Golden Rule, the Ten Commandments, or the Sermon on the Mount inspirational and worthy of devotion. Yet these statements of principle, like all others, require interpretation by reason and testing by experience.

In sum, assuming God exists, our moral principles, even if attributed to the divine, need to be evaluated. And if God does not exist, we may still commit ourselves to care for others. A world without God need not be a world without love.

---

13. Matthew 21:12.

19

A Religious Life

A COMMON SUPPOSITION IS that a religious life necessarily involves believing in God, doing what is right in order to serve God and hoping thereby to attain the bliss supposedly found in heaven. I propose instead that someone may lead a religious life without believing in God but by doing what is right in response to the needs of others and thereby potentially achieving the joys that can be found on earth.

For illustration, I turn to a Yiddish tale authored by I. L. Peretz, described by one notable critic as "arguably the most important figure in the development of modern Jewish culture."[1] To summarize the story would fail to do it justice, and so I present it in its entirety.

***

---

1. *The I. L. Peretz Reader,* ed. Ruth R. Wisse (New Haven and London: Yale University Press, 2002), xiii.

IF NOT HIGHER[2]

Early every Friday morning, at the time of the Penitential Prayers,[3] the rabbi of Nemirov[4] would vanish.

He was nowhere to be seen—neither in the synagogue nor in the two study houses nor at a minyan.[5] And he was certainly not at home. His door stood open: whoever wished could go in and out; no one would steal from the rabbi. But not a living creature was within.

Where could the rabbi be? Where should he be? In heaven, no doubt. A rabbi has plenty of business to take care of just before the Days of Awe.[6] Jews, God bless them, need livelihood, peace, health, and good matches. They want to be pious and good, but our sins are so great, and Satan of the thousand eyes watches the whole earth from one end to the other. What he sees, he reports; he denounces, informs. Who can help us if not the rabbi?

That's what the people thought.

But once a Litvak[7] came, and he laughed. You know the Litvaks. They think little of the holy books but stuff themselves with Talmud[8] and law. So this Litvak points to a passage in the Gemara—it sticks in your eyes—where it is written that even Moses our Teacher did not ascend to heaven during his lifetime but remained suspended two and a half feet below. Go argue with a Litvak!

So where can the rabbi be?

2. I. J. Peretz, "If Not Higher," trans. Marie Syrkin, from *The I. J. Peretz Reader*, 178–181. The accompanying notes are my own.

3. A type of liturgical poetry requesting forgiveness from sins.

4. A Ukrainian city with a flourishing Jewish community in the seventeenth century but also the scene of a ghastly massacre of the Jews by the Cossacks in 1648.

5. A group of ten male adult Jews, the minimum required for a communal prayer.

6. The ten-day period from Rosh Hashanah, the Jewish New Year, to Yom Kippur, the Day of Atonement.

7. A Jew from Lithuania.

8. The multi-volume compilation of Jewish law and commentary, containing the Mishnah, the core of the Oral Law, and the Gemara, a supplement to the Mishnah.

"That's not my business," said the Litvak, shrugging. Yet all the while—what a Litvak can do!—he is scheming to find out.

That same night, right after the evening prayers, the Litvak steals into the rabbi's room, slides under the rabbi's bed, and waits. He'll watch all night and discover where the rabbi vanishes and what he does during the Penitential Prayers.

Someone else might have gotten drowsy and fallen asleep, but a Litvak is never at a loss; he recites a whole tractate of the Talmud by heart.

At dawn he hears the call to prayers.

The rabbi has already been awake for a long time. The Litvak has heard him groaning for a whole hour.

Whoever has heard the rabbi of Nemirov groan knows how much sorrow for all Israel, how much suffering, lies in each groan. A man's heart might break, hearing it. But a Litvak is made of iron; he listens and remains where he is. The rabbi—long life to him!—lies on the bed, and the Litvak under the bed.

The Litvak hears the beds in the house begin to creak; he hears people jumping out of their beds, mumbling a few Jewish words, pouring water on their fingernails, banging doors. Everyone has left. It is again quiet and dark; a bit of light from the moon shines through the shutters.

(Afterward, the Litvak admitted that when he found himself alone with the rabbi a great fear took hold of him. Goose pimples spread across his skin, and the roots of his sidelocks pricked him like needles. A trifle: to be alone with the rabbi at the time of the Penitential Prayers! But a Litvak is stubborn. So he quivered like a fish in water and remained where he was.)

Finally, the rabbi—long life to him!—arises. First, he does what befits a Jew.[9] Then he goes to the clothes closet and takes out a bundle of peasant clothes: linen trousers, high boots, a coat, a big felt hat, and a long, wide leather belt studded with brass nails. The rabbi gets dressed. From his coat pocket dangles the end of a heavy peasant rope.

The rabbi goes out, and the Litvak follows him.

9. Morning prayers.

On the way the rabbi stops in the kitchen, bends down, takes an ax from under the bed, puts it into his belt, and leaves the house. The Litvak trembles but continues to follow.

The hushed dread of the Days of Awe hangs over the dark streets. Every once in a while a cry rises from some minyan reciting the Penitential Prayers, or from a sickbed. The rabbi hugs the sides of the streets, keeping to the shade of the houses. He glides from house to house, and the Litvak after him. The Litvak hears the sound of his heartbeats mingling with the sound of the rabbi's heavy steps. But he keeps on going and follows the rabbi to the outskirts of the town.

A small wood stands just outside the town.

The rabbi—long life to him!—enters the wood. He takes thirty or forty steps and stops by a small tree. The Litvak, overcome with amazement, watches the rabbi take the ax out of his belt and strike the tree. He hears the tree creak and fall. The rabbi chops the tree into logs and the logs into sticks. Then he makes a bundle of the wood and ties it with the rope in his pocket. He puts the bundle of wood on his back, shoves the ax back into his belt, and returns to the town.

He stops at a back street beside a small, broken-down shack and knocks at the window.

"Who is there?" asks a frightened voice. The Litvak recognizes it as the voice of a sick Jewish woman.

"I," answers the rabbi in the accent of a peasant.

"Who is I?"

"Again the rabbi answers in Russian, "Vassil."

"Who is Vassil, and what do you want?"

"I have wood to sell, very cheap." And not waiting for the woman's reply, he goes into the house.

The Litvak steals in after him. In the gray light of early morning he sees a poor room with broken, miserable furnishings. A sick woman, wrapped in rags, lies on the bed. She complains bitterly. "Buy? How can I buy? Where will a poor widow get money?"

"I'll lend it to you," answers the supposed Vassil. "It's only six cents."

"And how will I ever pay you back?" asks the poor woman, groaning.

"Foolish one," says the rabbi, reproachfully. "See, you are a poor, sick Jew, and I am ready to trust you with a little wood. I am sure you'll pay. While you, you have such a great and mighty God and you don't trust him for six cents."

"And who will kindle the fire?" asks the widow. "Have I the strength to get up? My son is at work."

"I'll kindle the fire," answers the rabbi.

As the rabbi put the wood into the oven he recited, in a groan, the first portion of the Penitential Prayers.

As he kindled the fire and the wood burned brightly, he recited, a bit more joyously, the second portion of the Penitential Prayers. When the fire was set, he recited the third portion, and then he shut the stove.

The Litvak who saw all this became a disciple of the rabbi.

And ever after, when another disciple tells how the rabbi of Nemirov ascends to heaven at the time of the Penitential Prayers, the Litvak does not laugh. He only adds quietly, "If not higher."

***

Those last three words embody an unusual view of the relationship between God and religion. If the Litvak believed in God and God's heaven, the Litvak could conceive nothing higher. His comment thus signifies a skeptical attitude toward traditional theism. Yet he becomes a follower of the rabbi because of admiration for the rabbi's ethical commitments and the extraordinary manner in which he fulfills them.

The rabbi is not without guile. He acts surreptitiously, dons a disguise, and speaks misleadingly to the distressed woman. The deceptions, however, serve a moral purpose, and in striving to do good, the rabbi is not bound by common conventions. He does not slavishly follow the law but seeks to embody its spirit.

The rabbi thereby captures the essence of a religion that can be embraced even by those who do not adopt orthodox theistic beliefs. It has its rituals and prayers, but these are valuable only insofar as they accompany noble deeds. Whether to affirm the existence of God or Satan is a metaphysical issue about which the rabbi and the Litvak may differ. (Who knows what the cunning rabbi believes?) The rabbi's eminence, though, rests not on the profundity of his theology but on the deep concern he shows for the sick and the poor. His wondrous actions leave the Litvak in awe of the rabbi's holiness.

Believing in God, the divine will, and the promise of eternal life are important aspects of many religions, but not all. The Litvak is a doubter but becomes a disciple. He laughs at the Bible but eventually reveres the rabbi. The Litvak scoffs at talk of heaven, but as events unfold, his understanding grows. In the end, the Litvak realizes that without ever leaving this world, the rabbi in his wisdom has found a way to deal with suffering and has attained a blessedness beyond any celestial vision of which human beings may dream.

Works by Steven M. Cahn

BOOKS AUTHORED

Fate, Logic, and Time. Yale University Press, 1967. Ridgeview Publishing Company, 1982. Wipf and Stock Publishers, 2004.

A New Introduction to Philosophy. Harper & Row, 1971. University Press of America 1986. Wipf and Stock Publishers, 2004.

The Eclipse of Excellence: A Critique of American Higher Education (Foreword by Charles Frankel). Public Affairs Press, 1973. Wipf and Stock Publishers, 2004.

Education and the Democratic Ideal. Nelson-Hall Company, 1979. Wipf and Stock Publishers, 2004.

Saints and Scamps: Ethics in Academia. Rowman & Littlefield, 1986. Revised Edition, 1994. 25th Anniversary Edition, 2011 (Foreword by Thomas H. Powell).

Philosophical Explorations: Freedom, God, and Goodness. Prometheus Books, 1989.

Puzzles & Perplexities: Collected Essays. Rowman & Littlefield, 2002. Second Edition, 2007

God, Reason, and Religion. Thomson/Wadsworth, 2006.

From Student to Scholar: A Candid Guide to Becoming a Professor (Foreword by Catharine R. Stimpson). Columbia University Press, 2008. Second Edition, Wipf and Stock Publishers, 2024.

Polishing Your Prose: How to Turn First Drafts Into Finished Work (with Victor L. Cahn). Foreword by Mary Ann Caws. Columbia University Press, 2013.

Happiness and Goodness: Philosophical Reflections on Living Well (with Christine Vitrano). Foreword by Robert B. Talisse. Columbia University Press, 2015.

Religion Within Reason. Columbia University Press, 2017. Second Edition, Wipf and Stock Publishers, 2025.

Teaching Philosophy: A Guide Routledge, 2018.

Inside Academia: Professors, Politics, and Policies. Rutgers University Press, 2019.

The Road Traveled and Other Essays. Wipf and Stock Publishers, 2019.

Philosophical Adventures. Broadview Press, 2019.

A Philosopher's Journey: Essays from Six Decades. Wipf and Stock Publishers, 2020.

Philosophical Debates. Wipf and Stock Publishers, 2021.

Navigating Academic Life: How the System Works. Routledge, 2021.

Professors as Teachers. Wipf and Stock Publishers, 2022.

Exploring Academic Ethics. Wipf and Stock Publishers, 2024.

BOOKS EDITED

Philosophy of Art and Aesthetics: From Plato to Wittgenstein (with Frank A. Tillman). Harper & Row, 1969.

The Philosophical Foundations of Education. Harper & Row, 1970.

Philosophy of Religion. Harper & Row, 1970.

Classics of Western Philosophy. Hackett Publishing Company, 1977. Second Edition, 1985. Third Edition, 1990. Fourth Edition, 1995. Fifth Edition, 1999. Sixth Edition, 2003. Seventh Edition, 2007. Eighth Edition, 2012.

New Studies in the Philosophy of John Dewey. University Press of New England, 1977.

Scholars Who Teach: The Art of College Teaching. Nelson-Hall Company, 1978. Wipf and Stock Publishers, 2004.

Contemporary Philosophy of Religion (with David Shatz). Oxford University Press, 1982.

Reason at Work: Introductory Readings in Philosophy (with Patricia Kitcher and George Sher). Harcourt Brace Jovanovich, 1984. Second Edition, 1990. Third Edition (also with Peter J. Markie), 1995.

Morality, Responsibility, and the University: Studies in Academic Ethics. Temple University Press, 1990.

Affirmative Action and the University: A Philosophical Inquiry. Temple University Press, 1993.

Twentieth-Century Ethical Theory (with Joram G. Haber). Prentice Hall, 1995.

The Affirmative Action Debate. Routledge, 1995. Second Edition, 2002

Classics of Modern Political Theory: Machiavelli to Mill. Oxford University Press, 1997.

Classic and Contemporary Readings in the Philosophy of Education. McGraw Hill, 1997. Second Edition, Oxford University Press, 2012.

Ethics: History, Theory, and Contemporary Issues (with Peter Markie). Oxford University Press, 1998. Second Edition, 2002. Third Edition, 2006. Fourth Edition, 2009. Fifth Edition, 2012. Sixth Edition, 2015. Seventh Edition, 2020.

Exploring Philosophy: An Introductory Anthology. Oxford University Press, 2000. Second Edition, 2005. Third Edition, 2009. Fourth Edition, 2012. Fifth Edition, 2015. Sixth Edition, 2018. Seventh Edition, 2021. Eighth Edition, 2024.

Classics of Political and Moral Philosophy. Oxford University Press, 2002. Second Edition, 2012.

Questions About God: Today's Philosophers Ponder the Divine (with David Shatz). Oxford University Press, 2002.

Morality and Public Policy (with Tziporah Kasachkoff). Prentice Hall, 2003.

Knowledge and Reality (with Maureen Eckert and Robert Buckley). Prentice Hall, 2003.

Philosophy for the 21st Century: A Comprehensive Reader. Oxford University Press, 2003.

Ten Essential Texts in the Philosophy of Religion. Oxford University Press, 2005.

Political Philosophy: The Essential Texts. Oxford University Press, 2005. Second Edition, 2011. Third Edition, 2015. Fourth Edition, 2022.

Philosophical Horizons: Introductory Readings (with Maureen Eckert). Thomson/Wadsworth, 2006. Second Edition, 2012.

Aesthetics: A Comprehensive Anthology (with Aaron Meskin). Blackwell, 2008. Second Edition (with Stephanie Ross and Sandra Shapshay), 2020.

Happiness: Classic and Contemporary Readings (with Christine Vitrano) Oxford University Press, 2008.

The Meaning of Life, 3rd Edition: A Reader (with E. M. Klemke). Oxford University Press, 2008. Fourth Edition, 2018.

Seven Masterpieces of Philosophy. Pearson Longman, 2008.

The Elements of Philosophy: Readings from Past and Present (with Tamar Szabó Gendler and Susanna Siegel). Oxford University Press, 2008.

Exploring Philosophy of Religion: An Introductory Anthology. Oxford University Press, 2009. Second Edition, 2016.

Exploring Ethics: An Introductory Anthology. Oxford University Press, 2009. Second Edition, 2011. Third Edition, 2014. Fourth Edition, 2017. Fifth Edition, 2020. Sixth Edition, 2023.

Philosophy of Education: The Essential Texts. Routledge, 2009.

Political Problems (with Robert B. Talisse). Prentice Hall, 2011.

Thinking About Logic: Classic Essays (with Robert B. Talisse and Scott F. Aikin). Westview Press, 2011.

Fate, Time, and Language: An Essay on Free Will by David Foster Wallace (with Maureen Eckert). Columbia University Press, 2011.

Moral Problems in Higher Education. Temple University Press, 2011. Wipf and Stock Publishers, 2021.

Political Philosophy in the Twenty-First Century (with Robert B. Talisse). Westview Press, 2013.

Portraits of American Philosophy. Rowman & Littlefield, 2013.

Reason and Religions: Philosophy Looks at the World's Religious Beliefs. Wadsworth/Cengage Learning, 2014.

Freedom and the Self: Essays on the Philosophy of David Foster Wallace (with Maureen Eckert). Columbia University Press, 2015.

The World of Philosophy. Oxford University Press, 2016. Second Edition, 2019.

Principles of Moral Philosophy: Classic and Contemporary Approaches (with Andrew T. Forcehimes). Oxford University Press, 2017.

Foundations of Moral Philosophy: Readings in Metaethics (with Andrew T. Forcehimes). Oxford University Press, 2017.

Exploring Moral Problems: An Introductory Anthology (with Andrew T. Forcehimes). Oxford University Press, 2018.

Philosophers in the Classroom: Essays on Teaching (with Alexandra Bradner and Andrew Mills). Hackett Publishing Company, 2018.

An Annotated Kant: Groundwork for the Metaphysics of Morals. Rowman & Littlefield, 2020.

The Democracy Reader: From Classical to Contemporary Philosophy (with Andrew T. Forcehimes and Robert B. Talisse). Rowman & Littlefield, 2021.

Academic Ethics Today: Problems, Policies, and Perspectives on University Life. Rowman & Littlefield, 2022.

Privacy (with Carissa Véliz) Wilkey-Blackwell, 2023.

Understanding Kant's Groundwork. Hackett Publishing Company, 2023.

Bronx Socrates: Portrait of a Legendary Teacher. Wipf and Stock Publishers, 2024.

About the Author

STEVEN M. CAHN IS Professor Emeritus of Philosophy at the City University of New York Graduate Center, where he served for nearly a decade as Provost and Vice President for Academic Affairs, then as Acting President.

He was born in Springfield, Massachusetts, in 1942. His younger years were devoted to music, and he studied piano with Herbert Stessin of the Juilliard School and the renowned chamber music artist Artur Balsam. He also became a professional organist, playing for synagogue services and studying under the tutelage of the well-known composer Isadore Freed. At his high school, Woodmere Academy (now Lawrence Woodmere Academy), he was principal clarinetist of the school's celebrated concert band.

After earning an AB from Columbia College in 1963 and PhD in philosophy from Columbia University in 1966, Dr. Cahn taught at Dartmouth College, Vassar College, New York University, the University of Rochester, and the University of Vermont, where he chaired the Department of Philosophy and led the successful effort to build what has remained one of the country's most highly rated undergraduate programs.

He served as a program officer at the Exxon Education Foundation, as Acting Director for Humanities at the Rockefeller Foundation, and as the first Director of General Programs at the National Endowment for the Humanities. He formerly chaired the American Philosophical Association's Committee on the Teaching of Philosophy, was the Association's delegate to the American Council of Learned Societies, and was longtime President of

ABOUT THE AUTHOR

the John Dewey Foundation, where he proposed and bought to fruition the John Dewey Lectures, now delivered at every national meeting of the American Philosophical Association.

He has presented numerous addresses at colleges and universities throughout the United States, including the first Naumberg Memorial Lecture at UCLA, the Minerva Lecture at Union College, the convocation address at Florida International University, and a keynote speech to the Kenan Convocation at the University of North Carolina at Chapel Hill. He has also spoken to many organizations, among them the College Entrance Examination Board, the American Board of Internal Medicine, the American Association of State Colleges and Universities, the National Association of Academic Affairs Administrators, and both the Northeastern and Midwestern Associations of Graduate Schools.

Dr. Cahn is the author of more than twenty books and editor of over fifty others. He has also served as general editor of four multivolume series: *Blackwell Philosophy Guides*; *Blackwell Readings in Philosophy*; *Issues in Academic Ethics,* and *Critical Essays on the Classics.*

His numerous articles have appeared in a broad spectrum of publications, including *The Journal of Philosophy*, *The Chronicle of Higher Education*, *Shakespeare Newsletter*, *The American Journal of Medicine*, *The New Republic*, and *The New York Times*.

A collection of essays written in his honor, edited by two of his former doctoral students, Robert B. Talisse of Vanderbilt University and Maureen Eckert of the University of Massachusetts Dartmouth, is titled *A Teacher's Life: Essays for Steven M. Cahn*. His professional autobiography appears in his book *The Road Traveled and Other Essays.*

Index

A
Abraham, bargaining with God, 53–54, 56, 65
All-good God. *See* Goodness
All He Ever Wanted (Shreve), 20
All-knowing God, 1, 5, 17, 52
All-powerful God, 1, 2, 10, 12, 21, 34, 35, 37
Amos, on will of God, 49
Attributes, of God: all-knowing, 1, 5, 17, 52; all-powerful, 1, 2, 10, 12, 21, 34, 35, 37; benevolence, 20–23; comfort, 32–33, 35; goodness, 1, 5, 10–11, 12, 14–16, 35, 37, 52; knowledge, 37; worship for, 52

B
Bargaining, with God: by Abraham, 53–54, 56, 65; Kaplan and, 56
Belief, in God: religious life without, 78; theism on, 1, 24, 34, 72
Benevolence: of God, 20–23

C
Cohen, Jack J., 62
Commandments, of God, 64–65; Ten Commandments, 74–76, 77
Confucius, 73

Cosmological argument, on existence of God, 1–2; defense of, 2–3; difficulty in, 3
cummings, e. e., 38

D
Darwin, Charles, 5
Death of God movement, 66
Deists, on revelations of God, 46
Demon, the, Zoroastrians on God's struggle with, 21
Descartes, René, 63
Despot, God analogy with, 55–56
Developer worship, God's worship compared to, 51–53
Dewey, John, 1, 63
Dialogues Concerning Natural Religion (Hume), 4, 18
Divine will. *See* Will, of God
Dummy hypothesis: benevolence of God, 20–23

E
Ecclesiastes, Book of, 19
Epicurus, 10, 14, 45
Ethics (Spinoza), 64
Euthyphro (Plato), 64
Evil: existence of, 10–13: method of negative theodicy, 10, 11–12, 32; moral evil, 11, 33; physical evil, 11

Existence, of God: cosmological argument on, 1–2; Kierkegaard on, 6; ontological argument on, 2–3; philosophical proofs for, 6–9; teleological argument on, 3–5; theism and, 1, 10, 18, 72; without proof, 47–49

Experience, of God: another's report of, 9; Hook on revelations of, 44; personal, 9, 44; philosophical doubts about, 9; Rowe on, 45

Ezekiel, 74–75

F

Faith: belief in, 24–26; skepticism about, 27–31

Frankel, Charles, 66

Franklin, Benjamin, 46, 48–49

Free will, 11, 15

G

Genesis, on worship of God, 53–54

Gershom, Levi ben. *See* Gersonides

Gersonides, 37

God: all-knowing, 1, 5, 17, 52; all-powerful, 1, 2, 10, 12, 21, 34, 35, 37; bargaining with, 53–54, 56, 65; belief in, 1, 24–26, 34, 72, 78; benevolence of, 20–23; commandments, of, 64–65, 74–76, 77; despot analogy to, 55–56; existence of, 1–5, 6–9, 32, 72, 77; experience of, 8–9, 44, 45; faith in, 24–26; goodness of, 1, 5, 7, 10–11, 12, 14–16, 32, 35, 37, 52; knowledge of, 36–39, 52; life and death control of, 54–55; life without, 72–77; meaning of, 1; moral standards of, 7–8, 65; mystery of, 29, 36; problem of meaning, 36–39; providence of, 26; relationship between religion, 82; religion without, 60–67; revelations of, 44–46; reverence of, 50–51; Satan's wager with, 30–31; Spinoza identification of Nature with, 64; theism on nature of, 34–35; theodicy on evil in plans of, 32–35; understanding of, 36; will of, 8–9, 40–43, 47–49, 54; without religion, 44–46; worship of, 48, 50–56; Zoroastrians on Demon struggle with, 21

Golden Rule, 73–74, 77

Goodness: of God, 1, 5, 10–11, 12, 14–16, 31, 32, 35; types of, 14–16

H

Heaven, 68–71

Hick, John: 14: method of negative theodicy, 11–12, 14, 15, 16; miracles, 43; moral evils, 33

Hillel the Elder, 73

Hook, Sidney, 44

Hume, David, 4, 5, 10, 18, 59

Huxley, Julian, 63

J

Jefferson, Thomas, 46

Job, Book of: challenge to faith, 27–31; mystery of God and, 29; Satan's wager with God in, 30–31; on understanding of God, 36

Justice concept: Abraham bargaining with God, 53–54; will of God and, 54–56

INDEX

K

Kant, Immanuel, 2
Kaplan, Mordecai M., 6, 56, 65
Kaufman, Walter, 74
Kierkegaard, Søren, 6
Knowledge, of God: Gersonides on, 37; God's worship and, 52; problem of meaning, 36–39; Soskice on metaphor for, 38; theism on God's nature, 34–35

L

Leibniz, Gottfried, 63
Life: after death, 12, 15–16; God's control of death and, 55–56
Life, without God: Golden Rule, 73; meaningfulness of, 72–73; moral principles, 73–77

M

Meaningfulness: of life without God, 72–73, making sense of, 36–39
Metaphor and meaning, 36–39
Miracles, 40–43
Moral goods, 14–16
Moral standards: of God, 7–8, 65
Moriarty hypothesis, 17–19, 21
Mystery, of God, 29, 36

N

Nature: Spinoza on God's identification with, 64; theism on God's, 34–35
Negative justification, method of, 15

O

Ontological argument, on existence of God, 2–3
Oracles of prophets, on will of God, 8

P

Pascal, Blaise, 47
Pascal's wager, 47
Peretz, I. L., 78
Philosophical proofs, for existence of God: belief without, 47; Kierkegaard on, 6, on murder, 7–8; religious commitment, 6–9
Physical goods, 14–19
Plato, 64
Power, theism on God's limited, 34–35
Prayer, concept of, 62–63
Presence of God experience, 8–9
Prophets, oracles on will of God, 8
Providence, of God, 26
Psalm 32, 32

R

Reed, Walter, 22
Religions: beliefs, 48–49; commitment to God's existence, 6–9; cultures, 59; differences, 57–59; God without, 47, 60–67; naturalistic, 62–63, 66; relationship between God, 82; supernatural religion, 62–63, 65–66; without God, 44–46
Religious life, without belief in God, 78
Revelations, of God: deists on, 46; Epicurus on, 45; Hook on, 44; testimony of, 44; Xunzi on, 45–46
Reverence of God, worship compared to, 50–51
Ritual, 60–62
Robinson, John A. T., 66
Rousseau, Jacques, 46
Rowe, William L., 45

INDEX

S
Satan, God's wager with, 30–31
Schopenhauer, Arthur, 50
Scientific hypothesis, contrasted with dummy hypothesis, 22–23
Sermon on the Mount, 76–77
Shreve, Anita, 20
Soskice, Janet Martin, 38
Soul:—breaking, 15–16;—making, 12
Spinoza, Baruch, 63
Swinburne, Richard, 33–34

T
Teleological argument, on existence of God, 3–5
Testimony: of revelations of God, 44
Theism: on belief in God, 1, 24, 36, 72; on benevolence of God, 20, 21; existence of God, 1, 10, 18, 32; on God's providence, 27–28, 32; on knowledge of God's nature, 37; on limited power of God, 35; on partial understanding of God, 36
Theodicy: described, 10–11; evil in God's plans, 32–35
Torquemada, Tomás de, 65

V
Voltaire, 46

W
Washington, George, 46
Will, of God, 44–45; Amos on, 49; contrary to expectations, 48; experiencing, 40–43; Franklin on, 48–49; holy books on, 8–9; justice concept, 53–55; personal independence, 48–49; presence of God experience, 8–9; prophets' oracles, 8
Worship, of God, 48–49, 50–56; Abraham bargaining with God, 53–54, 65; Book of Genesis on, 53–54; developer worship compared to, 51–53; God's attributes and, 52; God's life and death control, 55–56; praise compared to, 52; reverence compared to, 50–51; Sodom and Gomorrah, 54–55; theism and, 50

X
Xunzi, on revelations of God, 45–46

Z
Zoroastrians: on God and Demon struggle, 21